D0848790

Cerebral Hemisphere Function in Depression

The
PROGRESS IN PSYCHIATRY
Series

David Spiegel, M.D.,
Series Editor

Cerebral Hemisphere Function in Depression

Edited by
Marcel Kinsbourne, M.D.

1400 K Street, N.W.
Washington, DC 20005

Copyright © 1988 American Psychiatric Press, Inc.
ALL RIGHTS RESERVED
Manufactured in the United States of America
First Edition   88 89 90 91 5 4 3 2 1

The paper used in this publication meets the minimum requirements of American National Standard for Information Sciences—Permanence of Paper for Printed Library Materials, ANSI Z39.48-1984.   ∞

Library of Congress Cataloging-in-Publication Data

Cerebral hemisphere function in depression.

(The Progress in psychiatry series)
Includes bibliographies.
 1. Depression, Mental—Physiological aspects.
2. Cerebral hemispheres. 3. Cerebral dominance.
4. Brain—Localization of functions. I. Kinsbourne,
Marcel, 1931–   . II. Series. [DNLM: 1. Depression.
2. Dominance, Cerebral—physiology. WM 171 C414]
RC537.C44   1987   616.85′27   87-19304
ISBN 0-88048-143-9 (alk. paper)

Contents

vii   Contributors

ix   Introduction to the *Progress in Psychiatry* Series
David Spiegel, M.D.

xi   Introduction
Marcel Kinsbourne, M.D.

1   1   Cerebral Asymmetry, Affective Style, and Psychopathology
Richard J. Davidson, Ph.D.

23   2   Lateralized Emotional Response Following Stroke
Sergio E. Starkstein, M.D.
Robert G. Robinson, M.D.

49   3   Depressed Mood and Reduced Emotionality after Right-Hemisphere Brain Damage
Arnstein Finset, Ph.D.

65   4   Regional Brain Dysfunction in Depression
Bruce E. Wexler, M.D.

79   5   Cortical Activation in Psychiatric
             Disorder
             Frank B. Wood, Ph.D.
             Lynn Flowers, M.A.

99   6   Neuropsychological Mechanisms of
             Affective Self-Regulation
             Don M. Tucker, Ph.D.

133 7   Hemisphere Interactions in Depression
             Marcel Kinsbourne, M.D.

163 8   Conceptual and Methodological Issues
             in Neuropsychological Studies of
             Depression
             David Galin, M.D.

Contributors

Richard J. Davidson, Ph.D.
University of Wisconsin-Madison, Madison, Wisconsin

Arnstein Finset, Ph.D.
Sunnaas Rehabilitation Hospital, Nesoden, Norway

Lynn Flowers, M.A.
Bowman Gray School of Medicine of Wake Forest University,
Winston-Salem, North Carolina

David Galin, M.D.
Langley Porter Institute, University of California, San Francisco,
San Francisco, California

Marcel Kinsbourne, M.D.
Eunice Kennedy Shriver Center, Waltham, Massachusetts; and
Harvard Medical School, Boston, Massachusetts

Robert G. Robinson, M.D.
The Johns Hopkins University School of Medicine, Baltimore,
Maryland

Sergio E. Starkstein, M.D.
The Johns Hopkins University School of Medicine, Baltimore,
Maryland

Don M. Tucker, Ph.D.
University of Oregon, Eugene, Oregon

Bruce E. Wexler, M.D.
Yale University, New Haven, Connecticut

Frank B. Wood, Ph.D.
Bowman Gray School of Medicine of Wake Forest University,
Winston-Salem, North Carolina

Introduction to the Progress in Psychiatry Series

The *Progress in Psychiatry* Series is designed to capture in print the excitement that comes from assembling a diverse group of experts from various locations to examine in detail the newest information about a developing aspect of psychiatry. This series emerged as a collaboration between the American Psychiatric Association's Scientific Program Committee and the American Psychiatric Press, Inc. Great interest was generated by a number of the symposia presented each year at the APA Annual Meeting, and we realize that much of the information presented there, carefully assembled by people who are deeply immersed in a given area, would unfortunately not appear together in print. The symposia sessions at the Annual Meetings provide an unusual opportunity for experts who otherwise might not meet on the same platform to share their diverse viewpoints for a period of three hours. Some new themes are repeatedly reinforced and gain credence, while in other instances disagreements emerge, enabling the audience and now the reader to reach informed decisions about new directions in the field. The *Progress in Psychiatry* Series allows us to publish and capture some of the best of the symposia and thus provide an in-depth treatment of specific areas which might not otherwise be presented in broader review formats.

Psychiatry is by nature an interface discipline, combining the study of mind and brain, of individual and social environments, of the humane and the scientific. Therefore, progress in the field is rarely linear—it often comes from unexpected sources. Further, new developments emerge from an array of viewpoints that do not necessarily provide immediate agreement but rather expert examination of the issues. We intend to present innovative ideas and data that will enable you, the reader, to participate in this process.

We believe the *Progress in Psychiatry* Series will provide you with an opportunity to review timely new information in specific fields of interest as they are developing. We hope you find that the excitement of the presentations is captured in the written word and that this book proves to be informative and enjoyable reading.

David Spiegel, M.D.
Series Editor
Progress in Psychiatry Series

Introduction

Asurge of interest in biological psychiatry has swept into prominence a new area of scientific endeavor: the neuropsychology of psychopathology. Behavioral measures developed over a century to locate focal structural cerebral lesions and explicate their symptomatology now are being applied wholesale to patients with mental disorders. What motivates these efforts is obvious. If syndromes of mental disorder are really medical diseases, as the *Diagnostic and Statistical Manual of Mental Disorders (Third Edition) (DSM-III)* would have us believe, then one should be able to go beyond the surface phenomenology to identify some "biological marker" that is diagnostic of each disease. The hunt is on for biological markers in the various domains of psychopathology (smooth-pursuit eye movement deficit for schizophrenia), clinical chemistry (nonsuppression in the dexamethasone test for depression), pathological anatomy (multiple congenital anomalies for attention deficit disorder), and, pertinent to our inquiries, neuropsychological abnormalities construed to indicate cerebral dysfunction in various mental diseases. Since consensus on a biological marker is somewhat elusive for the other areas of analysis, can neuropsychology fill the gap? Is there some constellation of neuropsychological-test deficit and laterality-test outcome that differentially characterizes each of the major psychopathological entities?

The idea that cerebral dysfunction could be a marker for psychopathology arose from the fact that structural and functional cerebral disorders may mimic each other's symptoms. Patients with psychopathology were found to do poorly on certain neuropsychological tests that are known to indicate particular territories of cortical impairment in organic brain damage. Patients with brain damage were found to exhibit patterns of deviant affect, thought, and attention reminiscent of those that characterize the major psychopathologies. Perhaps, a reasonable argument goes, localization of function in the cerebral hemispheres applies not only to the cognitive variables traditionally studied, but also to parameters of attention, affect, and thinking that are central to psychiatric disease. Perhaps impairment ("dysfunction") of any one such area would deprive the individual of a particular contribution to his mental functioning, disinhibit other types of mental reactions, and additionally generate compensatory adjustments of behavior. In combination, such changes might account for the various behavioral symptom complexes that define the mental diseases.

A major research effort on the cerebral basis of emotion has provided normative underpinnings for such an approach (for instances, see chapters 1 and 6 in this volume). Evidence is rapidly accumulating that various parts of cerebral cortex play roles in controlling psychiatrically relevant behavioral parameters: the frontal lobes' involvement in impulse control and planning, the temporal lobes' involvement in adapting the individual's thoughts and actions to the realities of the environment, and the posterior parietal functions involved in identifying the emotional context within which the individual finds himself. Selective impairment of the future of any one of these areas could simulate, to a degree, aspects of such mental diseases as psychopathy, schizophrenia, and major affective disorder.

So far, the reasoning seems cogent. After all, the brain is the organ of the mind, and mental disorder must reflect deviant brain functioning (regardless of whether a biological or a dynamic account does more justice to the pathogenesis). But what can we expect to learn about psychopathology from cerebral functioning that is specifically useful?

A strong assumption could be that it is precisely the malfunction of a given cortical area that causes the psychopathology in the first place. The current data enable us neither to endorse nor dismiss this interpretation. The cause-effect relationships are unclear. Miscellaneous structural abnormalities are being reported both in schizophrenia and in affective disorder (e.g., Manschreck and Ames 1984), but the findings are nonspecific and of uncertain origin and certainly do not indicate focal cortical abnormality. Gross anatomy apart, what can we learn from "dysfunction"? If a person lacks a role model for impulse control, has dynamic reasons for disordered thinking, or reacts with depression to some adversity, then the attendant brain changes might represent the way in which such a person thinks, experiences events, and consequently controls his behavior. We might learn a good deal about which parts of the brain do what by studying such a person, but we would know nothing new about what causes mental disease.

Given that the strong hypothesis of a cerebral cause for mental disease lacks support, could the neuropsychological outcome nevertheless constitute a biological marker for the disease in question? Or could it be a marker indicating vulnerability to this disease given certain other necessary conditions?

Whether the neuropsychological concomitants of the various mental disorders are such trait markers is an empirical issue. It can only be resolved by showing that the neuropsychological finding antedates the origin of the disease clinically or persists during periods of remission, should these periods occur. Little of the available evidence is relevant to this issue. When it is, the neuropsychological findings are usually most parsimoniously regarded as state markers attending the mental disorder, rather than representing an enduring disease-related trait. Nor is it clear that a pattern of cerebral activation that occurs during an affective disorder is specific and therefore diagnostic of the disorder. Induced negative affect in normal people results in neuropsychological findings similar to some that are known to characterize depression (see Chapter 6).

Lowering our sights once again, can we hope at the very least that different neuropsychological constellations or outcomes will confirm the validity of the disease entities that we accept in our nosology, as in the *DSM-III* taxonomy? If each *DSM-III* entity were characterized by a distinctive cluster of neuropsychological findings, this would lend some validity to the particular classifications of mental disorders that *DSM-III* advocates. Alas, as discussed in Chapters 4 and 5, these entities are not necessarily characterized by such neuropsychological findings. Indeed, by adhering to certain *DSM-III* categories we may obscure rather than facilitate the drawing of biologically relevant neuropsychological distinctions.

Neuropsychological test patterns may ultimately turn out to offer everything for psychopathology that one might hope for—indications of causative cortical abnormalities, biological markers of malfunction representing trait rather than state, and validation of currently accepted psychiatric taxonomy. But whether they do this or not, there is another perhaps equally important reason for studying them. Beyond guiding us to locations in the brain that are instrumental in setting up deranged behavior, they may indicate the kind of brain mechanisms that we should attempt to model for purposes of understanding the origins and nature of psychiatric disease. Our current models, as befits the early stages of any line of scientific inquiry, are unduly simple. One-to-one correspondence between mental disease and focal cerebral dysfunction is unlikely. If a brain lesion results in depressive affect or in euphoria, the "explanation" that in the first case the lesion destroyed an area that inhibits depressive affect and in the second case an area that inhibits euphoria is circular and leads nowhere. Affective states are not the products of local cerebral activity. Instead, each affect is attended by a range of cognitive cerebral states. An analogous relationship obtains between one mental disease and one neurotransmitter function; that is, neither a specific, one state-one disorder relationship nor an orthogonal relationship across all disorders (Van Kammen 1987). Altered levels of a given neurotransmitter are associated with particular affective changes, but these associations apply across nosological entities. When drugs that alter levels of a particular neurotransmitter induce affective change, this change is not limited to one mental disease. If raising or lowering the level of a neurotransmitter corrects abnormal mental function, it does not follow that the mental abnormality was due to an abnormality in the neurotransmitter level. Neurotransmitter systems interact. The neurotransmitter change could be counteracting an abnormality inherent in another system.

Our goal is to clarify the functioning of brain areas and neurotransmitters as interacting systems that both generate change in mental states and react to changed mental states. This does not mean that the brain is impossibly complex. Complex it doubtless is, but some aspects of its function can be understood in simple terms. Positive and negative feedback loops are only minimally more complex than the arithmetic models that are in current vogue. There is much in psychopathology that arithmetic models do not explain. The extreme variability of behavior in schizophrenia and the effectiveness of treatments in decreasing that variability (Ploog 1950) are examples (see Chapter 4). Patterns of regional cerebral metabolism can vary wildly between patients within a disease category (see Chapter 5). Correspondence between a given psychoactive agent and a given mental disorder can be imperfect, to the point that agents with opposite effects on a given catecholamine system both may be beneficial to the same disease entity (Kinsbourne 1984). Conversely, the same agent can have opposite effects on different subjects (e.g., Mendenhall 1925; Kornelsky 1970). To quite an extent, the state of the organism determines the effect of the treatment, and that state is itself subject to variation induced by events impinging on the individual. Perhaps we should be thinking in terms of control systems (in their simplest form, opponent processors) that are subject to bias and to instability: Opponent systems are by no means confined to the cortex, but include cortical loci in their circuitry. The goal would be to develop an event-related flow chart of transactions in the brain as the organism reacts according to the well-known maladaptive patterns of mental disease. Observing such transactions might give a clearer picture of the nature of the disorder and monitoring them might be a better guide to effective treatment than the more gross and situationally confounded clinical phenomenology.

In the present volume we consider some steps toward a comprehensive neuropsychology of affective disorder. We consider information about changes in the physiological brain state associated with affective change in normal individuals (see Chapters 1 and 6); evidence about the involvements of various major cortical regions in affective disorder (see Chapter 4); and the patterns of structural cortical damage that generate behavior simulating depression (see Chapters 1 and 3). Finally we ponder methodological complexities that hamper interpretation of information in this field (see Chapter 8) and attempt to construct models for future research (see Chapters 6 and 7).

Marcel Kinsbourne, M.D.

REFERENCES

Kinsbourne M: Beyond attention deficit: search for the disorder in ADD, in Attention Deficit Disorder (I): Diagnostic, Cognitive, and Therapeutic Understanding. Edited by Bloomingdale LM. New York, Spectrum, 1984

Kornelsky C: Psychoactive drugs in the immature organism. Psychopharmacologia 17:105–136, 1970

Manschreck TC, Ames D: Neurologic features and psychopathology in schizophrenic disorders. Biol Psychiatry 19:703–720, 1984

Mendenhall WL: A study of tobacco smoking. Am J Physiol 72:549–557, 1925

Ploog D: "Psychische Gegenregulation" dargestellt am Verlaufe von Elektroschock Behandlungen. Archiv Psychiatrie Zeitschrift Neurologie 183:617–663, 1950

Van Kammen DP: 5-HT, a neurotransmitter for all seasons. Biol Psychiatry 22:1–3, 1987

Chapter 1

Cerebral Asymmetry, Affective Style, and Psychopathology

Richard J. Davidson, Ph.D.

Chapter 1

Cerebral Asymmetry, Affective Style, and Psychopathology

Although the role of the two cerebral hemispheres in cognition has been extensively studied over the past 20 years, comparatively little has been written on hemispheric function and emotion. Many factors are undoubtedly responsible for this state of affairs. Probably the most important, although least explicit, is the belief that the cortex does not have anything to do with emotion. Traditionally, the human cortex is viewed as the seat of higher cognitive functions. If any role is ascribed to the cortex in emotion, it is an inhibitory one, with cortical regions functioning to suppress subcortical limbic activity. This bias has crept into contemporary theorizing on the role of the two hemispheres in emotion (e.g., Levy 1983). More will be said about this issue later.

A second factor responsible for the relative lack of attention to emotion in studies of cerebral asymmetries is insufficient recognition of the importance of intrahemispheric specificity. Differences in functional specialization exist in different cortical regions along the rostral/caudal plane. Many of the asymmetries associated with language and other cognitive functions are mediated by posterior cortical areas (e.g., parietal and temporal regions). Recent findings in both normal subjects (e.g., Davidson 1984a) and brain-damaged subjects (e.g., Robinson et al. 1984) indicate that asymmetries related to the actual generation of emotion are localized in the anterior cortical regions. To tap asymmetries in these regions, methods other than standard behavioral paradigms involving dichotic listening and divided visual field presentations are required.

The research presented in this chapter was supported by National Institute of Mental Health grant no. MH40747, National Science Foundation no. BNS-8317229, and a grant from the Graduate School of the University of Wisconsin. Clifford Saron, Joseph Senulis, Andrew Tomarken, and Steven Zellmer contributed to the research.

Over the past 15 years, a growing body of literature has developed on cerebral asymmetries associated with emotion (for reviews, see Davidson 1984a; Silberman and Weingartner 1986; and Tucker 1981). Some controversy exists about the interpretation of the available evidence. In the next section, the adult data on asymmetry and emotion will be briefly summarized and the various interpretations that have been offered to explain these findings will be reviewed. Several of the current interpretive schemes will be shown to be seriously deficient, while those that offer the most promise will be highlighted. Emphasis will be placed on the individual differences in hemispheric activation and their relation to affective behavior in both normal subjects and subjects with affective disorders. The literature concerning adult subjects will be used to provide a context in which to examine the evidence on the development of emotion and its relation to cerebral asymmetry. Profound changes in emotional behavior naturally occur over the first 2 years of life and offer an ideal "model system" to study lateralization related to emotion. Moreover, individual differences in basic parameters of affect have been noted in very young infants. The relation between individual differences in activation asymmetries and affective responsiveness during the first year of life will be stressed.

LATERALIZATION OF EMOTIONAL FUNCTIONS: EVIDENCE FROM ADULT POPULATIONS

The data on the lateralizations of emotional functions come from several different sources. Perhaps the earliest references to asymmetries of this nature come from reports of the affective consequences of brain damage. Alford (1933) and Goldstein (1939) noted a high incidence of negative affect and "catastrophic" reactions among patients with unilateral left-hemisphere damage. A very different form of emotional reaction has been observed after unilateral damage to the opposite hemisphere. In patients with right-hemisphere damage, indifference or euphoria has been noted to predominate (for early reports see, e.g., Denny-Brown et al. 1952; Hecaen et al. 1951). Gainotti (1969, 1972) systematically compared the emotional behavior of patients with unilateral right- and left-sided lesions. He found that left-hemisphere lesions produced more frequent displays of the catastrophic reaction, while patients with right-hemisphere lesions showed a higher incidence of joking, indifference, and anosognosia. In a retrospective study of cases of pathological laughter and crying, Sackeim and associates (1982) found that left-sided lesions were more frequently associated with crying, whereas right-sided lesions were more often accompanied by laughing. In none of these studies was the location of the lesion within the hemisphere considered in the analyses.

An important series of recent studies has begun to systematically evaluate the effects of lesion location on affective behavior. Robinson and his colleagues, in a number of elegant studies, have found that the proximity of a left-hemisphere lesion to the frontal pole (assessed by computed tomography [CT] scan) is correlated with the severity of depressive symptomatology (Robinson and Benson 1981; Robinson and Szetela 1981; Robinson et al. 1984). The closer the lesion to the frontal pole, the more severe the depression. Among patients with left hemisphere lesions, Robinson et al. (1984) have reported a -0.54 correlation between distance of the lesion from the frontal pole and severity of depressive symptomatology (based upon a composite of several different indices). Out of the group of 30 patients studied by Robinson et al. (1984), 8 met Research Diagnostic Criteria for major depressive disorder. Among these 8 patients, 6 had left anterior lesions.

The association of frontal-lobe damage with affective disturbance is not surprising in light of the unique anatomical situation of this brain region. The frontal lobes have extensive anatomical reciprocity with various limbic structures directly implicated in the control of emotion (Nauta 1964, 1971). A variety of neuropsychological evidence links damage of particular frontal-lobe areas to deficits in affective regulation (e.g., Akert 1964; Luria 1966, 1973; Pribram 1973). In recent research, frontal-lobe lesions have been found to impair both voluntary and spontaneous facial expressions (Kolb and Milner 1981a, 1981b). For these and other reasons, the cortical region most likely to participate in the generation of emotional processes is the frontal region. As we note below, brain electrical activity recorded from this region is more consistently related to emotional behavior and experience than other cortical regions that have been sampled.

Several other lines of research with clinical populations support the differential lateralization of positive and negative affect. These include studies on the effects on mood of unilateral injections of sodium amytal, lateralized dysfunctions in patients with affective disorders, and the differential effects of left-sided versus right-sided electroconvulsive therapy. These data have been extensively reviewed in the past (e.g., Davidson 1984a) and are not considered here. In general, the evidence from these other sources has been found to be consistent with the findings from the brain damage data.

In normal subjects, a variety of procedures have been used to make inferences about underlying hemispheric asymmetries associated with emotion. A large body of literature on the perception of emotional information indicates that the right hemisphere, particularly the parietal region, plays an essential role in this process (see reviews by Bryden 1982; Etcoff 1986). Moreover, some workers have suggested that the right-hemisphere superiority in the perception of emotional information is independent of the more general superiority of this hemisphere in visuospatial tasks (e.g., Etcoff 1986). The superiority of the right hemisphere for tasks requiring the perception of emotional information has been attributed to an overall advantage of this hemisphere in the "processing" of emotion. As we underscore below, the posterior regions of the hemispheres actively participate in perceptual tasks, while the anterior regions have been implicated in tasks involving the generation of emotional expression. It is in the anterior regions, *when emotion is recruited*, that differential asymmetries as a function of affective valence have been observed.

One of the most effective ways to examine asymmetries in hemispheric activation during the generation of emotion is to record the electroencephalogram (EEG) in response to stimuli that elicit affect and assess asymmetries in activation as a function of the nature of the emotion that is elicited. This is a strategy that we have used extensively in both our adult and infant studies. In most of the studies described below, we compared asymmetries in the frontal and parietal scalp regions in response to stimuli that were designed to elicit a range of different positive and negative emotions. Based on the brain damage literature described above, we hypothesized that greater relative left-frontal than right-frontal activation would accompany epochs of positive affect compared with epochs of negative affect and vice versa. We also predicted that parietal asymmetry would not differentiate between positive and negative affect. In the adult studies, the major dependent variable has been power in the alpha (8–13 Hz) band. Decreases in power in this frequency band have been interpreted to reflect increased activation (Shagass 1972; Lindsley and Wicke 1974). Asymmetries in activation between the hemispheres have been examined by comparing alpha-band power derived from homologous electrode locations.

In our first study designed to evaluate EEG asymmetries associated with differential affective responses (Davidson et al. 1979a), 16 right-handed subjects were shown videotaped segments of popular television programs that were judged to vary in affective content. While viewing the videotape, subjects were instructed to continuously rate the degree to which they experienced positive versus negative affect by pressing up and down on a pressure-sensitive gauge. The output of this pressure transducer was digitized to provide a quantitative measure of affective self-report.

EEG was recorded from the left and right frontal (F3 and F4) and parietal (P3 and P4) regions referred to common vertex (Cz). Activity in the alpha band was extracted from the EEG, integrated, and digitized. Electro-oculogram was also recorded, and epochs confounded by eye-movement artifact were eliminated. To obtain an independent measure of the subjects' affective response to the video stimuli, two channels of facial electromyogram (EMG) were also recorded—from the zygomatic (smile muscle) and frontalis (muscle associated with tension and frowning) regions. EMG data were also integrated and digitized.

To test our major hypotheses, we compared the 30-second epoch *each subject* judged to be most positive with the one rated as most negative. This information was derived from the pressure transducer data. The positive and negative epochs deviated from the central neutral position by comparable amounts. We first compared the positive and negative epochs on an alpha laterality ratio score $(R - L/R + L$ alpha power). Higher numbers on this score indicate greater relative left-sided activation. We found significantly greater relative left-frontal activation during those epochs that subjects judged to be most positive compared with those they judged to be most negative. Parietal asymmetry did not discriminate between conditions. Analysis of the separate alpha power from the right- and left-frontal sites indicated that the difference between conditions was a function of changes in both hemispheres. Compared with the negative epochs, the positive epochs were associated with less left-frontal and more right-frontal alpha.

To confirm independently that the epochs subjects self-rated as positive and negative produced expressive changes consistent with these emotional shifts, we examined the integrated EMG recorded from the zygomatic and frontalis muscle regions. Positive segments elicited reliably more zygomatic and less frontalis activity than did negative segments.

We performed several other studies in adults using a variety of different affect elicitors and confirmed the basic effect described above (Bennett et al. 1982; Davidson et al. 1985). More recently, we have attempted to characterize more precisely the specific emotions which manifest the frontal asymmetry. Are they all positive and negative emotions, or a specific subset? Following Kinsbourne (1978), we proposed that the frontal asymmetry that we observed in the EEG was a reflection of a basic asymmetry for the control of approach versus withdrawal behavior. We argued that these behavioral systems require very different motor programming and that the motor specialization of the left hemisphere is uniquely suited for the control of approach, while that of the right hemisphere is appropriate for the control of withdrawal (see Davidson 1984a, 1984b for reviews of this argument). Based on this scheme, positive emotions that are accompanied by approach should be associated with left-frontal activation, while negative emotions accompanied by withdrawal should be associated with right-frontal activation. Certainly, not all negative emotions are regularly associated with withdrawal. For example, sadness may not elicit withdrawal. Anger is associated with approach when the angered individual strikes out at the object or person responsible for frustrating a sought-after goal. We reasoned that the emotions of disgust and fear would be those most likely associated with right-frontal activation because of their association with withdrawal behavior.

To explore this possibility, we embarked on a collaborative study (Davidson et al., in preparation). The purpose of the experiment was to expose subjects to films designed to elicit primarily happiness and disgust while brain activity was monitored (from the left and right frontal and parietal scalp regions) and the subjects' facial behavior was unobtrusively videotaped. In this experiment, we chose to use the face as a flag to specify epochs during which discrete facial signs of emotion were present. We would then examine the EEG during the display of expressions of happiness and disgust. The videotaped records were coded off-line using Ekman and Friesen's (1982) EMFACS system for the presence of discrete facial expressions of emotion. Onset and offset times for facial expressions of happiness and disgust were determined, and artifact-free EEG during those periods were extracted for analysis. The EEGs were Fourier-transformed, and power in the alpha band was computed. The data from this experiment supported our hypothesis. During facial expressions of disgust, there was significantly more relative right-frontal activation than with facial signs of happiness. No differences in parietal asymmetry were observed between emotions. As a control procedure, we extracted EEGs from the positive and negative films during periods in which no emotional facial behavior was occurring. No differences were found in asymmetry at either frontal or parietal sites between EEGs extracted during the periods from the positive film and those extracted during the periods from the negative film. In other words, the use of facial signs of emotion as a flag was quite fruitful in revealing those periods during which the EEG reflected differences caused by emotion.

EARLY SIGNS OF EMOTIONAL LATERALIZATION: EEG STUDIES OF AFFECTIVE PROCESSING DURING THE FIRST YEAR OF LIFE

In collaborative research with Nathan Fox, we have undertaken similar studies in infants. The initial purpose of these studies was to determine whether the frontal asymmetry observed in adults during certain positive and negative emotion conditions is also present in infants in the first year of life. In our first set of studies in this area (Davidson and Fox 1982), we decided to test 10-month-old infants since by this age, infants display facial signs of all the primary emotions (Campos et al. 1984). Two studies were conducted in which a videotape of an actress laughing and crying (the order was varied among subjects) was presented to the infants. The only difference between studies was that in the second, an experimenter monitored subjects' fixation on the video monitor and all the data analyzed derived only from those portions during which the infants were fixating. The infants sat on their mother's lap and watched the video monitor. The emotion segments (90 seconds in duration) were interspersed with portions of *Sesame Street*, which was used to capture the infants' attention. The audio portion of the videotape was edited to equate the happy and sad segments. Thirty-eight female infants (each born to two right-handed parents) were seen across two studies. Artifact-free EEGs were obtainable from 24 of these infants.

EEG was recorded from the left and right frontal and parietal regions (referenced to vertex) and stored on separate channels of FM tape. EEG in response to each segment from each of the four leads was reviewed and edited for gross eye movement and muscle and movement artifact. If artifact was present in any of the four channels, the data from *all four* channels were discarded, so that data from each of the four leads were always for coincident points in time. In these initial studies, artifact-free EEG was filtered for 1–12 Hz activity. The filtered output was then digitized, and energy (in uv sec) in this band was computed for each of the four leads separately for each of the conditions.

Laterality ratio scores ($R - L/R + L$, 1–12 Hz activity) were computed for frontal and parietal scalp leads for each of the two emotion conditions. The findings for the two studies were virtually identical, and the effects described below were independently significant for each experiment. As predicted, parietal asymmetry did not discriminate between the happy and sad segments. Similar to the findings for adults, the frontal ratio score did discriminate between conditions, with greater relative left-sided activation elicited in response to the happy segments and relative right-sided activation present in response to the sad segments (Table 1). When the contributions of the left-frontal and right-frontal regions were separately examined, it was found that the left hemisphere changed more than the right between conditions. The left hemisphere was more active during the happy than the sad segments. Across both studies, 20 of the 24 infants showed equal or greater relative left-frontal activation during the happy as compared to the sad epochs. These findings were the first to demonstrate that the frontal asymmetry for positive versus negative affect that was found in adults is present in infants in the first year of life.

While the data on 10-month-old infants described above suggest that the frontal asymmetry is "hard-wired," it is certainly possible that a considerable amount of learning relevant to emotion and its motor sequelae occurs during the first 10 months. In an attempt to extend the finding of frontal asymmetry differences between positive and negative affect back even earlier, we (Fox and Davidson 1986) performed a study with newborn infants. Thirty-three full-term, healthy infants, 2 to 3 days of age, were recruited from the newborn nursery of a large metropolitan hospital. All infants selected for participation in the study were born to two right-handed parents. In an effort to elicit approach and withdrawal reactions from newborns, we exposed the infants to different tastes presented via pipette on the tongue. Distilled water was first presented to acclimate subjects to the procedure. This was followed by a sucrose solution and then by citric acid. Infants' facial behavior was videotaped while EEG was recorded from the left and right frontal and parietal scalp regions according to the methods described above. Analysis of the videotapes indicated that facial signs of disgust were present in equal amounts in response to the initial introduction of water and to citric acid. EEG from these epochs revealed right-hemisphere activation (reductions in right-

Table 1. Mean (SD) frontal laterality ratio score by condition in two studies.

Study	No. of Subjects	Condition	
		Happy	Sad
1	10	0.021 (0.051)	−0.001 (0.032)
2	14	0.073 (0.100)	0.032 (0.115)

Note. Frontal laterality ratio score = F4 − F3/F4 + F3 1- to 12-Hz activity. Higher numbers indicate greater relative left-sided activation. Data from Davidson and Fox (1982).

hemisphere power in the 3- to 6-Hz and 6- to 12-Hz bands) in both regions in response to the water condition compared with the other two conditions. The sucrose condition produced greater relative left-sided activation in both regions compared with the water condition (see Table 2).

The findings from this study generally support the view that asymmetry of hemispheric activation in response to affective stimuli is present at birth. Unexpectedly, we found the greatest difference in EEG asymmetry between the responses to water and sucrose. We expected the water to be a neutral condition that would fall between the other two taste conditions. The facial data indicate that the water condition was associated with the display of disgust expressions. Perhaps this was because the water was always the first stimulus condition. Introducing a pipette into the infants' mouth may, in itself, be aversive. While this may explain right-sided activation for the water condition, it does not explain the lack of a right-sided effect for the citric acid condition, during which there also were facial signs of disgust. It is noteworthy that EEG during periods of movement artifact was excluded from analysis. In response to citric acid, much movement was elicited coincident with facial signs of disgust. The EEG during response to citric acid mostly consisted of periods following the cessation of both the movement and the disgust expression. Thus we probably did not capture for analysis those periods during which the strongest affective response occurred.

Unexpectedly, the right-sided activation in response to water con-

Table 2. Means and SDs for log power (in uV^2) in the 3- to 6-Hz band separately for the left-frontal and right-frontal and parietal regions, by condition.

Condition	Frontal		Parietal	
	Left	Right	Left	Right
Water				
Mean	0.35	−0.14	1.42	1.23
SD	1.42	1.55	0.96	1.01
Sugar				
Mean	0.44	0.70	1.06	1.38
SD	1.12	1.00	0.93	0.82
Citric				
Mean	0.33	0.34	1.42	1.39
SD	1.59	1.47	1.00	0.78

Note. Data are from Fox and Davidson (1986).

dition was found at both frontal and parietal scalp locations. The differentiated activation of different functional regions of cortex may not emerge until later in the first year of life. Measures of regional brain metabolism in human infants are consistent with this suggestion (Chugani and Phelps 1986).

INDIVIDUAL DIFFERENCES IN FRONTAL ACTIVATION ASYMMETRY: RELATION TO AFFECTIVE STYLE AND PSYCHOPATHOLOGY IN ADULTS AND INFANTS

Pronounced differences among individuals are typical in both EEG and behavioral measures of asymmetry. Levy (1983) has suggested that the diversity among dextrals in the magnitude and direction of asymmetries on behavioral measures of "cerebral lateralization" may reflect true variations in "patterns of asymmetric hemispheric arousal that were superimposed on a relatively invariant pattern of hemispheric specialization" (p. 476). Levy underscores the inconsistency between the percentage of subjects who would be expected to show left lateralization of verbal processing and the percentage who actually show right-field advantages for verbal material on dichotic and divided-visual-field tasks. She attributes this discrepancy to individual differences in asymmetric hemispheric arousal and infers the magnitude of such differences on the basis of behavioral asymmetries. Levy and her colleagues (1983) have reported strong relations between individual differences in "hemispheric arousal" and performance on a variety of tasks that are presumed to require different degrees of relative activation of the two hemispheres.

Asymmetries on EEG recordings provide a more direct method for inferring individual differences in hemispheric activation. Individual differences in EEG asymmetry are reliable over a 1- to 3-week period (Amochaev and Salamy 1979; Ehrlichman and Wiener 1979). Several investigators have reported that individual differences in resting EEG activation asymmetry recorded from the posterior scalp regions are related to performance differences on verbal and spatial cognitive tasks (e.g., Davidson et al. 1979b; Furst 1976; Glass and Butler 1977). For example, we (Davidson et al. 1979b) found that greater right parietal activation during rest was associated with better performance on a face recognition task. Measures of frontal EEG asymmetry from the same points in time were uncorrelated with cognitive performance.

Since our studies on emotion indicated that frontal asymmetries were related to the valence of affective responding, we examined whether individual differences in affective style were related to variations in resting frontal activation asymmetry. In our previous work, we found that frontal activation asymmetry discriminated between happy and sad emotional conditions. We therefore reasoned that individual differences in frontal asymmetry would be related to depressive affect. In our first attempt to explore this issue (Schaffer et al. 1983), subjects were selected on the basis of extreme scores on the Beck Depression Inventory. We compared depressed and nondepressed subjects on resting, closed-eye, frontal, and parietal activation asymmetry (based upon measures of alpha power) recorded before and after a series of experimental tasks that lasted approximately 2 hours. Frontal asymmetry discriminated between the depressed and nondepressed groups. The major difference between the groups consisted of less left-frontal activation among the depressed than among the nondepressed subjects. Parietal asymmetry recorded at the same points in time failed to discriminate between groups. These findings underscore the specificity of frontal asymmetry for affect and indicate that individual differences on this measure are related to affective style.

In more recent work with adults (Davidson and Tomarken, in preparation), we have found that individual differences in resting frontal asymmetry predict the intensity of response to emotional films. In a sample of 20 normal right-handed female subjects, relatively greater right-frontal activation during rest was significantly correlated with increased intensity of fear in response to films designed to elicit negative affect. This pattern was present in response to each of the two negative films which were presented ($r = -0.49$ and -0.45 for each of the two films). Parietal asymmetry from the same points in time was unrelated to subjects' rating of emotional intensity ($r = -0.16$ for both films). In addition to assessing self-reported emotion after each of the film clips, we also assessed subjects' emotional experience after each resting baselines to determine whether resting asymmetries are related to spontaneous emotion during the baseline periods themselves. We found that resting activation asymmetry was unrelated to emotion reported during the baseline period. Thus, the subjects who showed right-frontal activation during this time were not simply in a dysphoric mood when they arrived for the experiment. We were not able to discriminate between subjects with extreme right-frontal versus left-frontal activation on any emotional scale from the baseline ratings.

We have recently explored the relation between resting frontal asymmetries and affective behavior in infants (Davidson and Fox, submitted for publication). Resting EEG was recorded from the left-frontal and right-frontal and parietal scalp regions for a 30-second period for 19 normal 10-month-old infants (all born to two right-handed parents). The mother was present in the room during the baseline measurement. After this period, two standardized approach sequences were presented. In the first a stranger approached the infant (with mother present); the second approach consisted of the mother approaching. After the mother-approach sequence, the mother was instructed to turn around and leave the room. The duration of this period was 30 seconds unless the infant was judged by the experimenter to be extremely upset, at which time the trial was terminated by having the mother reenter the subject room and comfort her baby. The infant was videotaped during all periods of the experiment.

In response to the maternal separation period, we coded the presence or absence of crying. Of the 14 infants with usable EEG during the baseline period, 7 were coded as criers and 7 as noncriers during this period. We then examined the EEG during the baseline period to determine whether the criers could be discriminated from the noncriers. Asymmetries in the frontal and parietal region at each frequency (in 1-Hz bins) from 5 to 9 Hz were compared between criers and noncriers. This frequency range was chosen since most of the power in the infant EEG is found between these frequencies. We found a reliable difference between criers and noncriers in frontal asymmetry at 8 Hz. The criers displayed significantly more relative right-sided frontal activation during rest compared with the noncriers. No differences were obtained in parietal asymmetry between these groups. When the individual hemisphere data were examined, the difference between groups was present only in the left-frontal region. Noncriers showed more left-frontal activation (i.e., less power) than criers. In addition, the criers showed significantly more right-frontal than left-frontal activation, while the noncriers showed a nonsignificant trend in the opposite direction. Of the seven infants who cried in this situation, only one did not show absolute right-frontal activation during the baseline period. Table 3 presents the frontal baseline data separately by hemisphere for the criers and noncriers.

The infants' facial behavior during the baseline period was coded to ascertain whether those who subsequently cried in response to maternal separation were simply in a more dysphoric mood when they first arrived for the experiment. In that case, the frontal-asymmetry differences in the baseline period would be interpreted differently. This question is the same one that we asked about our adult data. In that case we examined whether resting frontal asymmetries were related to subjects' self-reported emotional experiences during the same resting period. Since this type of data is obviously unavailable in infants, we used facial behavior as an index of emotional reactivity. Table 4 presents the data on the duration of different

Table 3. Power density in the 8-Hz band (in uV²/Hz) for the left-frontal and right-frontal leads during the baseline period for the criers ($n = 7$) and noncriers ($n = 7$).

	Lead	
Group	Left Frontal	Right Frontal
Criers		
Mean	6.78	2.54
SD	3.83	1.22
Noncriers		
Mean	3.55	4.85
SD	1.77	2.99

Note. Data are from Davidson and Fox, submitted for publication.

Table 4. Mean duration in seconds of facial affect for criers ($n = 7$) and noncriers ($n = 7$) during the baseline period.

Facial Affect	Criers	Noncriers
Interest		
Mean	12.0	11.3
SD	9.4	7.8
No expression		
Mean	19.0	15.1
SD	6.4	8.9
Joy/surprise		
Mean	3.4	3.2
SD	4.0	3.2
Negative affect		
Mean	1.5	1.4
SD	1.1	1.3

Note. The no-expression category represents the mean number of seconds during which no facial signs of emotion were present. The negative-affect category represents the mean number of seconds during which facial signs of any of the negative emotions (anger, fear, distress, sadness, and disgust) were expressed. Data are from Davidson and Fox, submitted for publication.

emotional expressions coded during the baseline period for the infants who subsequently went on to cry and for those who did not cry in response to maternal separation. As can be seen from this table, there were no differences between criers and noncriers in the incidence of any of the emotion expressions coded during baseline.

The individual differences I have referred to above have all been in measures of resting EEG asymmetry. We have recently studied task-dependent EEG asymmetry in depressed and nondepressed subjects (Davidson et al. 1985). Among normal subjects, greater positive affect is reported in response to affective facial stimuli presented initially to the left-hemisphere (right visual field [RVF]) than to the right hemisphere (left visual field [LVF]) (Davidson et al., 1987). We used this paradigm with depressed and nondepressed subjects while recording EEG from the frontal and parietal regions. We replicated the effect we previously obtained in the normal subjects. Self-reports of happiness were greater in response to stimuli presented to the RVF than to the identical stimuli presented to the LVF. The depressed subjects showed the opposite effect. The frontal EEG data paralleled the self-reports. The depressed subjects showed greater left-frontal activation in response to LVF compared with RVF presentations, while the controls showed the opposite effect. Parietal EEG from the same points in time indicated that both groups showed left parietal activation in response to RVF presentations and right-parietal activation in response to LVF presentations. Thus, the depressed subjects showed opposite patterns of EEG asymmetry in the parietal and frontal regions while the normal subjects showed similar patterns. To explore this finding quantitatively, we computed within-subject correlations between frontal and parietal asymmetry. Of 10 depressed subjects, 7 showed inverse correlations between activation in these scalp regions, while only 1 nondepressed subject showed this effect. This difference between groups is significant ($p < 0.01$ by Fisher's exact test).

These findings are of interest in that they demonstrate different relations between frontal and parietal activation asymmetry in depressed and nondepressed subjects. The observation in the neuropsychological literature of a selective deficit on spatial cognitive tasks presumably mediated by the right hemisphere (e.g., Flor-Henry et al. 1983) may be explained by our findings. We have established that depressed subjects have greater relative right-sided frontal activation compared with controls, which in turn may be associated with right parietal inhibition. Posterior right-sided inhibition may be the immediate cause of the performance deficit observed in these patients on cognitive tasks mediated by the right hemisphere.

WHAT DO FRONTAL ACTIVATION ASYMMETRIES REFLECT?

The data reviewed in the first two sections of this chapter indicate that differences in frontal activation asymmetry are observed in response to stimuli that elicit certain positive and negative emotional reactions. The data reviewed above indicate that right-frontal activation might occur during resting baseline conditions when neither self-report nor facial behavior indicates that negative emotion is present. In these circumstances, relative right-sided resting frontal activation was found to predict the intensity of the subsequent response to negative affective elicitors. Thus, the combination of available evidence indicates that under certain circumstances, right-frontal activation is associated with concurrent negative affect and in other circumstances it is not. This pattern of findings leads to the proposal that right-frontal activation is necessary but not sufficient for the experience of certain negative emotions. The presence of right-frontal activation might represent a "vulnerability" for the experience of negative emotion. The threshold for eliciting negative affect might be lower in this situation. Given a moderately intense negative stimulus, we would predict that those subjects with baseline right-frontal activation would respond more intensely compared with subjects displaying left-frontal activation. A weak negative stimulus should be capable of eliciting negative affect only among those who are relatively vulnerable. Subjects with strong left-frontal activation may represent an "invulnerable" group that requires an extremely intense elicitor to trigger negative affect.

Precisely why subjects with right-frontal activation should be more vulnerable to the experience of negative affect is not currently known. It may be that such subjects appraise situations differently than those not so affected. Perhaps appraisal is the same in both types of subjects, but the magnitude of response differs. Subjects with strong right-frontal activation may appraise the situation as only mildly stressful yet not be capable of regulating their extreme response. For example, in response to the negative films in one of our adult studies, a subject might report that she knew that the sequence was a film and objectively there was nothing to be scared of, yet she could not help herself and experienced a very strong reaction. Yet another possibility is that subjects with both left- and right-sided resting frontal activation appraise the situation similarly and respond with similar intensity. What distinguishes the subjects in this version is the availability of coping responses among those with left-frontal activation. These subjects may be able quickly to terminate their reaction, while subjects with right-frontal activation may lack the requisite coping skills to minimize the duration of the negative affective response.

The choice among these alternative explanations of what individual differences in resting frontal activation asymmetry actually reflect calls for research specifically designed to answer this question. Such investigation will require accurate measures of appraisal and coping processes, as well as the duration and intensity of the emotional reaction in question. The complexity in the interpretation of individual differences in resting frontal activation asymmetries underscores the relevance of basic emotion theory to studies on psychophysiological responses to emotional stimuli. It is clear that emotion is a multicomponential set of phenomena that can only be unraveled by careful attention to its differentiated nature. This requires a detailed examination of relations between physiological changes and specific emotion subcomponents.

SUMMARY AND CONCLUSIONS

In this chapter, selected findings on the lateralization of emotion in adults and infants have been reviewed. The importance of the distinction between perception and production of emotion was made at the outset. It was suggested that overall right-hemisphere superiority (across valence) is present for the perception of emotion, but that once emotion is recruited, differential lateralization of certain positive and negative emotions is found. This differential lateralization is most prominently observed in recordings of brain electrical activity from the frontal region. We have proposed, following Kinsbourne (1978), that the fundamental continuum along which the anterior regions of the hemispheres are lateralized for emotion is approach and withdrawal. In a study in which EEG was extracted during facial signs of emotion, we found that facial signs of disgust, unlike facial signs of happiness, were associated with right-frontal activation. We performed a series of studies in infants that demonstrate that the asymmetry for positive and negative emotion is present within the first year of life and probably at birth.

Pronounced individual differences are present in resting and task-dependent measures of EEG activation asymmetries. We have presented a series of findings in both adults and infants that indicate that resting EEG differences among subjects are related to differences in emotional style or reactivity. Adult subjects scoring high on the Beck Depression Inventory have decreased left-frontal activation during rest compared with nondepressed controls. In another study, we found that greater right-frontal activation during rest was correlated with increased intensity of self-reported fear in response to films designed to elicit negative affect. Among 10-month-old infants, those with resting right-frontal activation were more likely to cry in response to brief maternal separation than were those with left-frontal activation during rest. In the latter two studies, measures of affect during the baseline periods themselves were unrelated to resting frontal activation asymmetries. Finally, in examining task-dependent changes in frontal and parietal EEG asymmetry in depressed and nondepressed subjects, we found that depressed subjects showed reciprocal relations between activation asymmetry in these scalp regions, while control subjects showed positive correlations.

The findings reported in this chapter provide the basis for the assertion that the presence of right-frontal activation increases vulnerability to certain forms of negative affect. Precisely what the frontal asymmetry represents requires additional research that systematically disentangles the subcomponents of emotion and relates them to EEG measures. Appraisal and coping are two candidate subcomponents that may be related to the frontal asymmetries we have reported. It is clear that future research in this area must draw upon the sophistication that is now available both in behavioral studies of emotion and in cerebral psychophysiology.

REFERENCES

Akert K: Comparative anatomy of frontal cortex and thalamofrontal connections, in The Frontal Granular Cortex and Behavior. Edited by Warren JM, Akert K. New York, McGraw-Hill, 1964

Alford LB: Localization of consciousness and emotion. Am J Psychiatry 12:789–799, 1933

Amochaev A, Salamy A: Stability of EEG laterality effects. Psychophysiology 16:242–246, 1979

Bennett J, Davidson RJ, Saron C: Patterns of self-rating in response to verbally elicited affective imagery: relation to frontal vs. parietal EEG asymmetry. Psychophysiology 18:158, 1981

Bryden MP: Laterality: Functional Asymmetry in the Intact Brain. New York, Academic Press, 1982

Campos J, Barrett KC, Lamb ME, et al: Socioemotional development, in Handbook of Child Psychology, Volume 11. Edited by Hussen PH. New York, Wiley, 1983

Chugani HT, Phelps ME: Maturational changes in cerebral function in infants determined by 18FDG positron emission tomography. Science 231:840–843, 1986

Davidson RJ: Affect, cognition and hemispheric specialization, in Emotion, Cognition and Behavior. Edited by Izard CE, Kagan J, Zajonc R. New York, Cambridge University Press, 1984a

Davidson RJ: Hemispheric asymmetry and emotion, in Approaches to Emotion. Edited by Scherer K, Ekman P. Hillsdale, NJ, Erlbaum, 1984b

Davidson RJ, Fox NA: Asymmetrical brain activity discriminates between positive versus negative affective stimuli in human infants. Science 218:1235–1237, 1982

Davidson RJ, Fox NA: Resting patterns of brain electrical asymmetry predict infants' response to maternal separation. Manuscript submitted for publication

Davidson RJ, Tomarken AJ: Resting anterior EEG asymmetry predicts reactivity to affective films. Manuscript in preparation.

Davidson RJ, Schwartz GE, Saron C, et al: Frontal versus parietal EEG asymmetry during positive and negative affect. Psychophysiology 16:202–203, 1979a

Davidson RJ, Taylor N, Saron C, et al: Hemisphericity and styles of information processing: individual differences in EEG asymmetry and their relationship to cognitive performance. Psychophysiology 16:197, 1979b

Davidson RJ, Schaffer CE, Saron C: Effects of lateralized stimulus presentations on the self-report of emotion and EEG asymmetry in depressed and nondepressed subjects. Psychophysiology 22:353–364, 1985

Davidson RJ, Mednick D, Moss E, et al: Ratings of emotion in faces are influenced by the visual field to which affective information is presented. Brain and Cognition 6:403–411, 1987

Davidson RJ, Ekman P, Saron C, et al: EEG asymmetry during facial expressions of happiness and disgust. Manuscript in preparation

Denny-Brown D, Meyer ST, Horenstein S: The significance of perceptual rivalry resulting from parietal lesion. Brain 5:433–471, 1952

Ehrlichman H, Wiener MS: Consistency of task-related EEG asymmetries. Psychophysiology 16:247–252, 1979

Ekman P, Friesen WV: Felt, false and miserable smiles. Journal of Nonverbal Behavior 6:238–252, 1982

Etcoff NL: The neuropsychology of emotional expression, in Advances in Clinical Neuropsychology. Edited by Goldstein G, Tarter RE. New York, Plenum Press, 1986

Flor-Henry P, Fromm-Auch D, Schopflocher D: Neuropsychological dimensions in psychopathology, in Laterality and Psychopathology. Edited by Flor-Henry P, Gruzelier J. New York, Elsevier, 1983

Fox NA, Davidson RJ: Hemispheric substrates of affect: a developmental model, in The Psychobiology of Affective Development. Edited by Fox NA, Davidson RJ. Hillsdale, NJ, Erlbaum, 1984

Fox NA, Davidson RJ: Taste-elicited changes in facial signs of emotion and the asymmetry of brain electrical activity in human newborns. Neuropsychologia 24:417–422, 1986

Furst CJ: EEG asymmetry and visuospatial performance. Nature 260:254–255, 1976

Gainotti G: Reactions "Catastrophiques" et manifestations d'indifférence au cours des atteintes cerebrales. Neuropsychologia 7:195–204, 1969

Gainotti G: Emotional behavior and hemispheric side of lesion. Cortex 8:41–55, 1972

Glass A, Butler SR: Alpha EEG asymmetry and speed of left hemisphere thinking. Neurosci Lett 4:231–235, 1977

Goldstein K: The Organism. New York, Academic Books, 1939

Hecaen H, Ajuriaguerra JD, Massonet J: Les troubles visuoconstructifs par lesions parieto-occipitales droites: roles des pertubations vestibulaires. L'Encephale 1:122–179, 1951

Kinsbourne M: Biological determinants of functional bisymmetry and asymmetry, in Asymmetrical Function of the Brain. Edited by M. Kinsbourne. New York, Cambridge University Press, 1978

Kolb B, Milner B: Performance of complex arm and facial movements after focal brain lesions. Neuropsychologia 19:491–503, 1981a

Kolb B, Milner B: Observations on spontaneous facial expression after focal cerebral excisions and after intracarotid injection of sodium amytal. Neuropsychologia 19:505–514, 1981b

Levy J: Individual differences in cerebral hemisphere asymmetry: theoretical issues and experimental considerations, in Cerebral Hemisphere Asymmetry: Method, Theory and Application. Edited by Hellige JB. New York, Praeger, 1983

Levy J, Heller W, Banich MT, et al.: Are variations among right-handed individuals in perceptual asymmetries caused by characteristic arousal differences between the hemispheres? J Exp Psychol [Hum Percept] 9:329–359, 1983

Lindsley DB, Wicke JD: The electroencephalogram: autonomous electrical activity in man and animals, in Bioelectric Recording Techniques. B. Electroencephalography and Human Brain Potentials. New York, Academic Press, 1974

Luria AR: Higher Cortical Functions in Man. New York, Basic Books, 1966

Luria AR: The Working Brain. New York, Basic Books, 1973

Nauta WJH: Some efferent connections of the prefrontal cortex in the monkey, in The Frontal Granular Cortex and Behavior. Edited by Warren JM, Albert K. New York, McGraw-Hill, 1964

Nauta WJH: The problem of the frontal lobe: a reinterpretation. J Psychiat Res 8:167–187, 1971

Pribram KH: The primate frontal cortex-executive of the brain, in Psychophysiology of the Frontal Lobes. Edited by Pribram KH, Luria AR. New York, Academic Press, 1973

Robinson RG, Benson DF: Depression in aphasic patients: frequency, severity and clinical-pathological correlations. Brain Lang 14:282–291, 1981

Robinson RG, Szetela B: Mood change following left hemispheric brain injury. Ann Neurol 9:447–453, 1981

Robinson RG, Kubos KL, Starr LB, et al: Mood disorders in stroke patients: importance of location of lesion. Brain 107:81–93, 1984

Sackeim HA, Weinman AL, Gur RC, et al: Pathological laughing and crying: functional brain asymmetry in the experience of positive and negative emotions. Arch Neurology 39:210–218, 1982

Schaffer CE, Davidson RJ, Saron C: Frontal and parietal EEG asymmetries in depressed and non-depressed subjects. Biol Psychiatry 18:753–762, 1983

Shagass C: Electrical activity of the brain, in Handbook of Psychophysiology. Edited by Greenfield NS, Sternbach RH. New York, Holt, Rinehart and Winston, 1972

Silberman EK, Weingartner H: Hemispheric lateralization of functions related to emotion. Brain and Cognition 5:322–353, 1986

Tucker DM: Lateral brain function, emotion and conceptualization. Psychol Bull 89:19–46, 1981

Chapter 2

Lateralized Emotional Response Following Stroke

Sergio E. Starkstein, M.D.
Robert G. Robinson, M.D.

Chapter 2

Lateralized Emotional Response Following Stroke

As early as the nineteenth century, clinicians such as Broca (1861) and Wernicke (1874) identified language and behavioral disturbances associated with unilateral cerebral lesions. This was the earliest recognition that the cerebral hemispheres of the human brain were not simply redundant symmetrical structures in their behavioral response to injury; rather, each hemisphere played a specialized, unique role in the production of behavior. Since that time, much information about lateralized hemispheric specialization has emerged.

Babinski (1922) reported anosognosia, euphoria, and indifference after right hemisphere lesions. Hecaen et al. (1951) and Denny-Brown et al. (1952) described the indifference reaction, which features anosognosia or anosodiaphoria, lack of interest, and inappropriate jocularity as its main symptoms. Goldstein (1942) described the catastrophic reaction associated with left-hemisphere (LH) damage. He regarded the catastrophic reaction as an explosive emotional response of brain-damaged patients to cognitive tasks that exceed their abilities.

Lateralization of emotional response due to unilateral hemisphere inactivation, however, was first described by Terzian and Cecotto (1959), who reported that the catastrophic reaction was produced by LH inactivation with an intracarotid amytal injection, while euphoria was elicited after right-hemisphere (RH) inactivation. Although other investigators also have reported similar responses to carotid amytal injection (Perria et al. 1961; Alema and Rossadini 1964), this reaction has not always been found (Tsunoda and Oka 1976; Milner 1974).

Lateralization of emotional response, however, has been most extensively studied after unilateral cerebral lesions. Sackheim et al. (1982) observed that while pathological laughing was associated with

25

RH damage, pathological crying was related to left-side damage. They noted that patients with right cerebral hemispherectomy showed high positive affect and also reported that gelastic epileptic outbursts were more common in patients with a left-sided foci on electroencephalogram (EEG), while dacrystic epileptic ictus was more frequently observed in patients with right-sided foci.

Gainotti (1969, 1972) was the first to address the issue of emotional symptoms associated with brain injuries in a systematic study. He found that while catastrophic reactions were significantly more frequent in LH-damaged patients, the indifference reaction (anosognosia and anosodiaphoria, misoplegia, and jocular behavior) was clearly associated with RH damage (Gainotti 1972). He considered the catastrophic reaction as an appropriate emotional reaction to the severe verbal and right-sided motor disorders, while he explained the indifference reaction as secondary to a strong need for denial of illness (Gainotti 1983).

Although most investigators explained catastrophic and depressive symptoms as a psychological reaction of the organism confronted with a severe cognitive disability (Fisher 1961; Borden 1968), systematic studies have consistently failed to find a strong association between post-brain injury depression and severity of physical disability (Folstein et al. 1978; Gasparrini et al. 1978; Finkelstein et al. 1982). Folstein et al. (1978) studies depression in 20 stroke and 10 orthopedic patients with the same level of functional disability and found more depression in the stroke group. Gasparrini et al. (1978) studied 24 brain-damaged patients, 16 with LH and 8 with RH lesions, using the Minnesota Multiphasic Personality Inventory (MMPI). Of the 10 MMPI scales, only the depression scale showed a significant difference between RH- and LH-damaged patients. While 45 percent of LH-damaged patients scored in the abnormal range, none of the RH-damaged patients scored abnormally. This difference could not be explained by motor or cognitive impairment, and the authors also stressed the fact that, as the MMPI is not modified by abnormalities in affective intoned speech, prosodic disturbances could not explain the above findings. Finkelstein et al. (1982) assessed depression in randomly selected stroke patients and in a group of physically impaired nonstroke controls. While the two groups did not differ in the severity of their physical impairment, a significantly higher prevalence of depression was observed in stroke patients as compared to controls (46 versus 0 percent), and the prevalence tended to be higher in patients with LH rather than with RH lesions. Recently, de Bonis et al. (1985) also found more depression in patients with left-sided damage as compared to patients with RH lesions.

In summary, although lateralization of emotion, as demonstrated by unilateral cerebral inactivation or lesion studies, has been reported for many years, the emotional abnormality was generally assumed to be secondary to the physical or cognitive deficits elicited by the brain injury itself. Systematic studies, however, have not supported this assumption and have led to alternative explanations for lateralized emotional response to brain injury.

LATERALIZED MOOD DISORDERS AFTER STROKE

During the past several years we have been investigating the occurrence of mood disorders after cerebral ischemia (Robinson and Price 1982; Starkstein et al. 1987; Robinson et al. 1983, 1984a, 1984b). In one of these studies, we examined a group of 36 right-handed patients with ischemic or hemorrhagic stroke and without previous personal or family history of psychiatric disease, alcohol or drug abuse, evidence of previous brain injury by clinical history or computed tomography (CT) scan examination, decreased level of consciousness or severe comprehension deficits (Robinson et al. 1984a). Patients were selected if they had a lesion on CT scan that was localized to only one hemisphere. This enabled us to control for important variables such as lesion volume or location that could influence our findings. The psychiatric examination included the Hamilton Depression Scale (Hamilton 1960), the Zung Depression Scale (Zung 1965), and the modified Present State Exam (Wing et al. 1974). We had shown in our previous studies that these scales were capable of providing reliable measurement of depression in this brain injured population (Robinson et al. 1983). On CT scan, lesion localization was calculated as follows: the lesion was considered anterior if its anterior border was rostral to 40 percent of the anterior-posterior distance and the posterior border was anterior to 60 percent of that distance. On the other hand, a lesion was considered posterior if its anterior border was posterior to 40 percent of the anterior-posterior distance and the posterior border was caudal to 60 percent of that distance.

Depression was determined by the existence of diagnostic symptom criteria from the *Diagnostic and Statistical Manual of Mental Disorders (Third Edition) (DSM-III)* for either major depression or minor (dysthymic) depression. Although the time criteria of 2 weeks' duration of symptoms for major depression and 2 years' duration of symptoms for dysthymic depression were not met in every case, patients were classified according to major and minor depression to determine whether the factors associated with depression were the same for different severities of depression.

When the hemispheric (right versus left) localization of the lesion was considered, depression (major or minor) was found in 14 of 22 patients with LH lesions, while only 2 of 14 patients with RH lesions were depressed. Using χ^2 analysis, a hypothesis of unequal frequency of distribution of depression based on the hemispheric lesion location was statistically substantiated ($\chi^2 = 9.4$, $df = 1$, $p < 0.01$). In addition to the importance of *inter*hemispheric lesion location in the frequency of depression, the *intra*hemispheric lesion location also was found to be important. For those patients whose lesions could be classified as either anterior or posterior, 7 of 10 patients with left-anterior lesions had depression (6 major and 1 minor), while only 3 of 8 patients with left-posterior lesions, 0 of 6 with right-anterior lesions, and 1 of 6 with right-posterior lesions were depressed ($\chi^2 = 8.22$, $df = 3$, $p < 0.05$) (Table 1). On the other hand, while 6 of 14 patients with right hemisphere lesions showed undue cheerfulness, none of the 22 patients with LH lesions showed that abnormal behavior ($\chi^2 = 8.6$, $df = 1$, $p < 0.01$). We also have recently demonstrated that subcortical as well as cortical lesions show the same lateralized and interhemispheric association with mood disorders (Starkstein et al. 1987). That is, left-anterior subcortical lesions are significantly more commonly associated with major depression than any other subcortical lesion location.

In summary, for a selected group of patients with single lesions of the right or left hemisphere and no known risk factors for depressive disorder, we found a lateralized emotional response to stroke. Left-anterior cortical or subcortical lesions were associated with depression, particularly major depression, while right-anterior hemisphere lesions were associated with inappropriate cheerfulness and apathy.

VARIABLES THAT AFFECT LATERALIZATION

Several investigators have examined the issue of lateralization of depression following stroke. Although most studies have reported depression and catastrophic reactions associated with LH lesions and cheerfulness or indifference associated with RH lesions, some investigators have failed to find this lateralized response. For instance, Folstein et al. (1978) found no difference in depression between RH and LH stroke patients although RH lesion patients showed more irritability. Sinyor et al. (1986) also found no difference in severity of depression between RH and LH lesion patients.

Table 1. Intrahemispheric Lesion Location and Psychiatric Diagnosis

Psychiatric Diagnosis	Left Hemisphere (n)		Right Hemisphere (n)	
	Anterior (10)	Posterior (8)	Anterior (6)	Posterior (6)
Major depression	6	1	0	1
Minor depression	1	3	0	1
Hypomania (Present State Exam)	0	0	5	1
None	3	4	1	3

Note. Reproduced from Robinson et al. (Brain 107:81, 1984); reprinted with permission.

The question thus arises of why some investigators have demonstrated a lateralized emotional response to brain injury while others have not. Although this question cannot be answered completely, our studies have suggested some variables that may be involved. In the previously cited study in which we showed statistically significant evidence of lateralized response to cerebral infarction, patients with previous personal history of affective disorder or alcoholism or family history of affective disorder were excluded. Thus, these factors, which could put someone at risk for developing poststroke depression but were not controlled for by these other investigators, may have contributed to these other investigators' inability to find a lateralized response to focal brain injury.

Another variable that may contribute to why some investigators find lateralization and some do not is lesion location. As indicated in the previous section, our studies have demonstrated that *intra*hemispheric as well as *inter*hemispheric lesion location is important in determining type and severity of mood disorders after stroke (Robinson et al. 1984a). In fact, in the initial evaluation of 103 patients included in a 2-year longitudinal study of poststroke mood disorders that we have conducted, we did not find significant differences in severity of depression between LH and RH lesion patients until we compared left-frontal-lobe lesion patients with RH lesion patients (Robinson et al. 1983). In other words, when we did not control for factors such as prior history of psychiatric disorder or the anterior-posterior location of the ischemic injury, lateralization of emotional response could not be demonstrated. Anterior lesions produced a more strongly lateralized emotional response than posterior lesions, and it was only when we invoked this more "powerful" factor that we demonstrated lateralization.

Another important factor influencing whether studies find lateralized emotional response to brain injury is prior brain injury. In a study of 15 patients with bilateral brain injury (Lipsey et al. 1983), we found that severity of depression was related only to LH brain damage. Patients with left-frontal injury were significantly more depressed than those with left-posterior damage, and this was independent of location of the RH lesion or temporal sequence of lesions (see Figure 1). The implications of this finding for studies of lateralization are that, if a patient has an old left-frontal lesion perhaps not even visualized on CT scan and subsequently has a new RH stroke, that patient's depressive symptoms will be related to the location of the old LH lesion. This could easily confound studies of lateralization if prior brain injury is not taken into account and the location of the prior stroke determined.

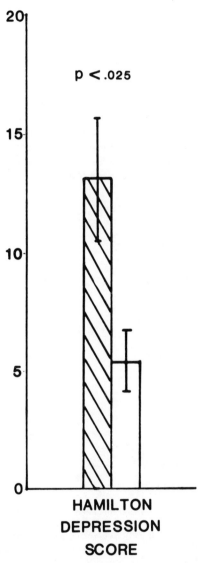

Figure 1. Hamilton depression scores for patients with left anterior lesions (hatched bars) and patients without left anterior lesions (open bars). Higher scores indicate more severe depression (bars indicate ± SEM). Reproduced from Lipsey et al. (Br J Psychiatry 143:266, 1983); reprinted with permission.

Another important variable is time elapsed since brain injury. We have reported (Robinson et al. 1983, 1984a) that during the acute stroke period, lesion location was the variable that showed the strongest correlation with severity of depression (i.e. left anterior lesions produced the most severe depressions) (see Figure 2). This relationship also was observed at both 3 and 6 months poststroke. For patients with RH lesions, however, we found that the distance of the lesion from the frontal pole was positively correlated with severity of depression during the acute poststroke period (Robinson et al. 1984a). That is, lesions *farthest* from the frontal pole were associated with the most severe depressions (see Figure 2). At 6-month followup, however, the trend of this correlation reversed, so that the

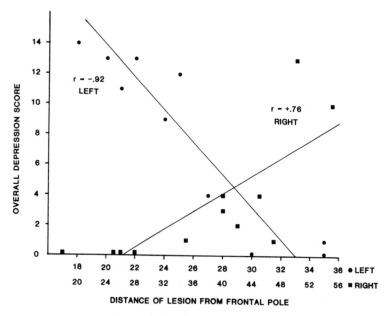

Figure 2. Relationship between overall depression score and distance of the anterior border of the lesion from the frontal pole for patients with either left anterior hemisphere infarcts or right hemisphere infarcts. The distance from the frontal pole is expressed as a percentage of the total anteroposterior distance. The correlation coefficients are indicated in the figure; r left, $p<0.001$; r right, $p<0.01$. Reproduced from Robinson et al. (Brain 107:81, 1984); reprinted with permission.

distance of the lesion from the frontal pole correlated inversely with severity of depression. That is, lesions *closest* to the frontal pole were associated with the most severe depressions (i.e., the same relationship as found with LH lesions) (Robinson et al. 1984a). This temporal change in the relationship between lesion location and severity of depression after RH stroke may explain why some authors (Folstein et al. 1978; Sinyor et al. 1986) who have assessed chronic stroke patients could not find differences in the incidence and severity of depression between those with LH lesions and those with RH lesions.

In summary, several variables appear to play important roles in the expression of lateralization of emotional response to brain injury. *Intra*hemispheric lesion location has a major effect on emotional response, with frontal lobe lesions producing the strongest evidence of lateralization. In addition, prior brain injury, personal or family history of psychiatric disorder, and time since stroke can also influence the lateralized response to stroke. Clearly, other investigators who are examining lateralized emotional changes need to control for these variables before any conclusions can be drawn about whether RH or LH brain injury lead to lateralized emotional response.

RESPONSE TO TREATMENT

Both major and minor depressions are common complications of stroke, occurring in approximately 30 to 60 percent of poststroke patients (Robinson et al. 1983, 1984b). In a longitudinal study of poststroke emotional disorders, we examined a consecutive series of 146 patients admitted to hospital for stroke. Although 43 had to be excluded because of decreased level of consciousness or severe comprehension deficits, among the remaining 103 patients, 27 percent had the symptom cluster of major depression and 20 percent had the symptom cluster of minor (dysthymic) depression (25 percent) (Robinson et al. 1983).

Thus, almost half of this consecutive series of interviewable stroke patients were clinically depressed. Based on the annual incidence for stroke of approximately 400,000 (Wolf et al. 1977), the need to evaluate effective and rapid treatment methods for poststroke depression is clear. We therefore evaluated the efficacy of nortriptyline, a tricyclic antidepressant, in a randomized, double-blind, placebo-controlled study that included patients with thromboembolic stroke or intracerebral hemorrhage (Lipsey et al. 1984). Fifty percent of the 34 patients who completed this study met *DSM-III* criteria for major depression, while the other half met the *DSM-III* symptom criteria for dysthymic (minor) depression. Although an expected initial improvement in depression scores was observed in the placebo group ($n = 20$), they showed no further improvement after the first 2 weeks; however, the nortriptyline-treated group ($n = 14$) continued to improve throughout the 6-week treatment period and were significantly better than the placebo group by the end of the study (see Figure 3). Patients were started on a 20-mg oral dose at bedtime. For weeks 2 and 3 the dose was increased to 50 mg. Patients were given 70 mg for week 4 and 100 mg for weeks 5 and 6. Of 17 patients on nortriptyline, 3 developed delirum with decreased level of consciousness, necessitating discontinuation of their medication. Patients with significant cardiac conduction delay, narrow-angle glaucoma, or prostatism with urinary obstruction were excluded from the study. Apart from delirium, complications (for example, worsening of cardiac status or subsequent stroke) in the actively treated

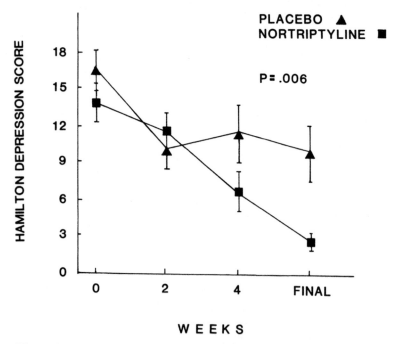

Figure 3.   Hamilton depression scores for nortriptyline and placebo groups over time. Higher scores indicate more severe depression; bars represent ± SEM. *P* values shown are derived from repeated measures analysis of variance of treatment and time interaction. Reproduced from Lipsey et al. (Lancet 1:297, 1984c); reprinted with permission.

group were no more frequent than in the placebo group. Elderly patients with multiple medical problems, however, need to be monitored carefully. Because the nortriptyline-treated group was a relatively small one, we could not determine whether patients with left-anterior lesions showed a different response to treatment with antidepressants than did patients with other lesion locations. Clearly, however, patients with LH lesions as well as patients with RH stroke improved with nortriptyline.

Several authors have reported on the importance of biogenic amine neurotransmitters depletion in the etiology of depression (Bunney and Garland 1981; Schildkraut 1965; Hoes 1985). This may also prove true for poststroke depression. In fact, we have demonstrated that small frontal cortical lesions produce widespread depletions of biogenic amines in the injured as well as the uninjured cerebral hemisphere of the rat (Robinson 1979; Robinson and Coyle 1980; Pearlson and Robinson 1981). As tricyclic antidepressants block the reuptake of noradrenaline and serotonin (Hollister 1978), the amelioration of poststroke depression could be secondary to the correction of stroke-induced changes in biogenic amines.

MECHANISMS OF LATERALIZED RESPONSE TO INJURY

A major reason for studying mood disorders after brain injury is the possibility of learning something about mood regulation in normal patients or the mechanisms leading to mood disorders in non-brain-injured patients. Although it is uncertain whether the mechanisms of poststroke depression and functional (non-brain-injured) depression are similar, the idea that studying brain-injured patients may provide some insight into the mechanisms of "functional" affective disorder has a precedent. Much of our understanding of mechanisms and localization of cognitive and language functions is based on lesion studies. The suggestion that depression after brain injury may share some of the same mechanisms as functional affective disorder would also be supported by finding that similar hemispheric asymmetries were related to both functional depressive disorders and poststroke depressive disorders.

In previous sections of this chapter, we have described the lateralized emotional response to stroke. In addition, several authors (Gruzelier and Venables 1973; Gruzelier and Venables 1974; Myslobodsky and Horesh 1978; Toone et al. 1981) studying patients with functional (non-brain-injured) depressions have reported lower right-hand than left-hand skin conductance response in depressed patients. In addition, asymmetrical responses in patients with endogenous depression also have been observed in conjugate lateral eye movement. Shifts in gaze to the left or right are normally related to a greater arousal of the contralateral hemisphere (Tucker 1981; Kinsbourne 1972). Thus, LH activation through verbal material produces a rightward deviation while leftward movements are obtained when the right hemisphere is aroused through visuospatial problems (Sandel and Alcorn 1980). Depressed patients without brain injury were found to show a bias toward looking left (Tucker 1981). Although this finding was explained as secondary to a RH hyperexcitability (Tucker 1981; Bryden 1982), the contrary (that is, a left hypoarousal) is also possible.

Baxter et al. (1985) measured cerebral metabolic rate using Positron Emission Tomography scanning (PET scan) in 11 patients with unipolar depression and found that the metabolic rate in the left frontal cortex was lower than that of the right frontal cortex in 3 of these patients. Moreover, patients with unipolar depression had a significantly lower caudate/hemisphere metabolic ratio as compared to controls, while on recovery the index returned toward control levels. Phelps et al. (1983) also reported on patients with unipolar depression who had asymmetrical PET scans showing decreased glucose metabolism in the left frontal region. After methylphenidate challenge, the asymmetry disappeared, only to increase later when mood worsened again.

Thus, although we do not know if functional and poststroke depressive disorders share any neurophysiological mechanisms or relate to the same anatomical structures, some findings suggest that there may be some overlap and that studies of brain-injured patients may be helpful in elucidating the mechanisms of function in affective disorders.

Interhemispheric Interaction

Based in part on the evidence that suggests that the two hemispheres may subserve different functions in mood regulation, several authors have postulated that in normal persons the left hemisphere processes positive emotions while the right hemisphere is more involved in negative affect (Bryden 1982). The association between left-anterior lesions and severe depression is therefore explained as a "release" phenomena. The LH lesion removes inhibition from the "depressive prone" right hemisphere, thus allowing the appearance of depression. If this assumption is correct, patients with bilateral lesions would not be expected to develop depression, or at least depression due to an LH lesion might be less severe after an RH lesion.

To test this hypothesis and to assess the hemispheric interdependence in mood regulation, we studied patients with bilateral lesions due to thromboembolic stroke, intracerebral hemorrhage, or focal traumatic brain injury (Lipsey et al. 1983). Based on the location of the most recent lesion (i.e., right, left, or simultaneous bilateral), we were unable to distinguish among groups in terms of severity of depression. When we grouped patients based on the location of the LH lesion regardless of the temporal sequence of right and left lesions, however, we found that patients with left-anterior lesions were significantly more depressed (see Figure 1). In fact, five of nine patients with left-anterior lesions were severely depressed, whereas none of the six patients with left-posterior lesions showed depression. Moreover, a significant inverse correlation between depression scores and the distance of the LH lesion from the frontal pole was found. For RH lesions, no significant correlation was observed between lesion location and depression scores.

In conclusion, this study of patients with bilateral injury not only replicated our previous findings of significantly more severe depression in patients with left-anterior lesions, but also demonstrated that in patients with bilateral hemispheric lesions, LH lesions are dominant in the induction of depression, regardless of the temporal sequence of brain damage. This study did not support the hypothesis that contralateral hemispheric "release" is an important mechanism in the development of poststroke depression.

Although hemispheric interaction is an important mechanism in many cognitive functions, a lack of interhemispheric interaction has also been observed by investigators studying other lateralized functions. Levine and Mohr (1979) for instance found that in four patients with bilateral brain damage, recovery of language after lesions appeared to be mediated by the surrounding structures of the left hemisphere, and not by the contralateral analogous area. Other investigators, however, have found evidence of RH involvement and recovery from LH language disorders (Levine and Mohr 1979).

Watson et al. (1984) studied left multimodal neglect in monkeys after a right-frontal ablation. They posed the thesis that if interhemispheric inhibition occurs after a unilateral hemispheric lesion, the injured hemisphere would not be able to inhibit the uninjured one, while the intact hemisphere would continue to inhibit the injured one. In this situation, a callosal section would cancel the last interaction. Watson et al. (1984) produced RH lesions in monkeys with 3-month-old callosal sections. If the uninjured left hemisphere was causing neglect through inhibition of the right hemisphere, monkeys with a callosal section would develop less neglect than monkeys with an intact corpus callosum. They found that monkeys with a callosal section performed even worse than the monkeys with an intact corpus callosum. They also noted that callosal-sectioned monkeys recovered completely from neglect, thus suggesting that recovery is mediated by *intra*hemispheric rather than *inter*hemispheric mechanisms. It is possible, however, that interhemispheric interaction could have taken place at the brainstem level, thus producing neglect, and that the decline in performance in the monkeys with a callosal section was because of another mechanism.

We also have examined the issue of interhemispheric interactions using laboratory animal studies. Bilateral cortical suction lesions in rats were produced either simultaneously or first in the left and then in the right hemisphere. Rats with bilateral lesions, regardless of the temporal sequence of lesions, developed the same behavioral abnormality (i.e., spontaneous hyperactivity) as did rats with only RH lesions (Dewberry et al. 1986). In addition, rats given corpus callosum sectioning as neonates and unilateral cortical suction lesions as adults were spontaneously hyperactive only if the right hemisphere had been injured (Dewberry et al. 1986). This study suggests that lateralized hyperactivity induced by right frontolateral cortical lesions does not rely on interhemispheric release or interaction. It also demonstrates that the appearance of the behavioral abnormality does not depend on the lesion sequence, but only on the disruption of unilateral intrahemispheric mechanisms.

Biogenic Amine Mechanisms

Although the mechanisms leading to the lateralized emotional response to stroke are only speculative, we have proposed a role for catecholamine-containing neurons.

The norepinephrine- and serotonin-containing pathways arise from the brainstem and project anteriorly into the frontal cortex and then pass anterior to posterior, running through the deep layers of the cortex and arborizing throughout the cortex (Morrison et al. 1979) (see Figure 4). Focal injury such as stroke may cause partial damage to catecholamine-containing neurons. Several investigators have demonstrated that catecholamine concentrations are significantly altered after stroke in humans (Meyer et al. 1973).

Reis et al. (1978) have suggested that injured catecholaminergic neurons may switch from producing neurotransmitter to synthesizing protein for regeneration and sprouting. This may lead to a precipitous decline in available transmitter throughout the injured as well as uninjured branches of the system. Using animal models of stroke, it has been shown that a focal cortical lesion can produce widespread

depletions of biogenic amine neurotransmitters throughout uninjured as well as injured areas of the brain (Robinson 1979; Robinson
and Coyle 1980; Zervas et al. 1974). We have suggested that this
widespread depletion of norepinephrine throughout the brain may
be expressed emotionally as major depression or perhaps cheerfulness
and apathy.

In addition, lateralized differences in the emotional response to
left-anterior brain injury (major depression) as compared with right-
anterior brain injury (indifference and apathy) may be the result of

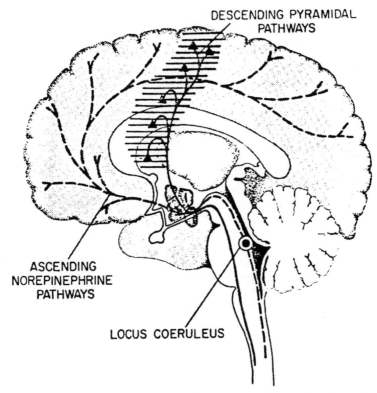

DESCENDING PYRAMIDAL
PATHWAYS

ASCENDING
NOREPINEPHRINE
PATHWAYS

LOCUS COERULEUS

Figure 4. Schematic drawing of the ascending noradrenergic pathways in
the human brain. Axonal projections pass into the frontal pole
and travel through the deep cortical layers with arborizations
into more superficial layers. This anatomy might explain why
anterior lesions produce more severe mood disorders than posterior lesions. Reproduced from Robinson and Bloom (Biol
Psychiatry 12:669, 1977); reprinted with permission.

differential biochemical responses to ischemia depending on which hemisphere is injured. In fact, after right middle cerebral artery ligations in rats, depletion of norepinephrine concentrations was observed within the ipsilateral and contralateral cortex, as well as the ipsilateral and contralateral locus coeruleus (Robinson 1979).

On the other hand, after left middle cerebral artery ligation, there were no postoperative changes in catecholamine levels (Robinson and Coyle 1980; Robinson et al. 1980). Thus, the biochemical response of the brain can be different depending on which hemisphere is injured. This suggests that the lateralized emotional response to injury found in stroke patients may be related to a differential biochemical response of the human brain to injury. RH lesions that lead to widespread depletion of norepinephrine concentrations may be expressed behaviorally as undue cheerfulness and apathy, while LH lesions (perhaps through depletion of another transmitter, such as serotonin) may lead to depression.

Intrahemispheric Mechanisms

Although exceptions may be found (Basso et al. 1985; Vignolo et al. 1986), specific neuropsychological syndromes are generally associated with the disruption of specific cortical areas (Damasio and Geschwind 1985). This has been referred to as topographical localization and has been very useful in localizing lesions of the central nervous system. For mood disturbances, however, that kind of localization has not been very useful. In fact, although there is a strong association between left-anterior lesions and the development of depression, no specific left-frontal cortical area has been found responsible for that behavioral/emotional manifestation. In several studies, however, we found a graded relationship between severity of depression and proximity of the lesion to the frontal pole (Robinson et al. 1984a). In other words, in addition to finding a lateralized emotional response to stroke, we (Robinson et al. 1984a) found that among patients with LH stroke, the closer the lesion was to the frontal pole, the more severe was the depression. We have suggested that this "graded localization" may be a consequence of the anatomy of the biogenic amine pathways.

Since noradrenergic axons arborize as they pass anteriorly to posteriorly through the deep layers of the cortex, a lesion in the anterior region of the brain would interrupt these pathways in a more "upstream" position and thus cause far greater disruption of transmitter concentrations than a posterior lesion, which would be more "downstream" (see Figure 4). This might lead to a graded effect of lesion location on norepinephrine concentrations and perhaps on depression or apathy. This anatomical relationship between anterior-posterior lesion location and depletion of biogenic amines might explain the clinical finding that the closer the lesion is to the frontal pole, the more severe the depression. In fact, we have observed in laboratory animals that an anterior hemispheric cerebral lesion causes greater disruption of noradrenergic transmitter concentrations than does a more posterior one (Pearlson and Robinson 1981). Thus, if mood is influenced by injury to these pathways, a "graded" effect, depending on the proximity of the lesion to the frontal pole, might be expected.

Role of Cerebral Dominance

If the mechanisms relating to lateralized mood response after brain injury are influenced by abnormalities in functions such as language or motor dominance, mood disorders in stroke patients with RH cerebral dominance might be altered. In addition, even if poststroke mood disorders have their own neurophysiological mechanisms, perhaps the anatomical substrates would change hemispheres in some patients related to cerebral dominance. We studied 30 left-handed patients who were hospitalized for stroke (Robinson et al. 1985). All the patients reported the dominant use of their left eye, left hand (for writing and eating), and left foot. We found that all of the depressed patients had an LH lesion and nondominant hand impairments with the exception of one patient with major depressive symptoms who had an RH lesion and dominant hand impairments. Of the 18 patients with LH lesions, 8 were not depressed, while 11 of 12 patients with RH lesions were not depressed. Depression scores on both the Present State Exam and the Zung Depression Scale were significantly higher in the patients with LH lesions than in those with RH lesions ($p<0.025$ and $p<0.01$, respectively) (see Figure 5). When patients were divided according to anterior and posterior lesion location, six of eight patients with left-anterior brain injury had major depression, while the other two had minor depression. Of the seven patients with left-posterior lesions, one patient had major depression, another had minor depression, and the last five were not depressed. Thus, in spite of the fact that they had nondominant motor impairments, LH lesion patients were significantly more depressed than RH lesion patients with dominant symptoms. In addition, among patients with left-anterior lesions, the proximity of their lesions to the frontal pole on CT scan correlated positively with severity of depression. This study suggests that the neurophysiological processes leading to poststroke depressive disorders may be independent of motor dominance and depend on the location of the LH lesion. It also suggests that the neuroanatomical structures important in mediating this poststroke mood disorder may be more "primitive" than cortical structures important in language and perhaps involve subcortical structures which preceded language development.

SUMMARY AND DIRECTIONS OF FUTURE RESEARCH

We have described a lateralized emotional response to brain injury: left-frontal stroke leads to major depression while right-frontal stroke leads to apathy and undue cheerfulness. Although the association

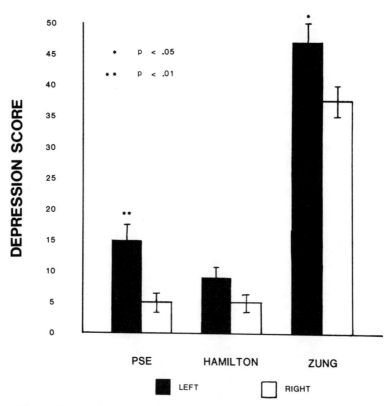

Figure 5. Relationship between depression and lesion hemisphere in 30 left-handed patients. PSE, Present State Exam. Reproduced from Robinson et al. (Am J Psychiatry 142:1424, 1985); reprinted with permission.

between LH lesions and depression as well as the development of flat affect and undue cheerfulness after RH lesions have been well demonstrated by many previous investigators using different methodologies, our work has emphasized the importance of intrahemispheric lesion location and the strong correlation between proximity of the lesion to the left-frontal pole and severity of depression. This lateralized emotional response to injury may be influenced by previous personal history of emotional disorder, previous brain injury, location of brain injury, or time since stroke and does not appear to be a manifestation of RH release (i.e., disinhibition). Although it is uncertain whether pharmacotherapy may be helpful for treatment of apathy, depressive disorders can be successfully treated with the tricyclic antidepressant nortriptyline. Laboratory experiments in rats have demonstrated that hyperactivity and widespread depletions of norepinephrine after RH anterior lesions occurred while identical lesions of the left hemisphere produced neither changes in spontaneous activity nor norepinephrine concentrations. This lateralized biochemical response to experimental stroke in the rat suggested that the lateralized mood disorders after stroke in humans may be mediated through asymmetrical alterations in biogenic amine neuronal pathways.

Future research may include studying poststroke psychopathology by means of improved imaging with nuclear magnetic resonance scanning or chemical investigation of the living brain using PET scan. The identification of lateralization in both rats and humans, as well as the work of other investigators showing lateralization through all orders of animal phylum, however, underlines the fundamental importance of lateralization in the organization of the nervous system and demonstrates the importance of asymmetrical neural mechanisms for behavior and perhaps mental states.

REFERENCES

Alema G, Rossadini G: Donnes cliniques et EEG de la introduction d'amytal sodium dans la circulation encephalique, concernant l'etat de conscience. Acta Neurochir (Wien) 12:240–257, 1964

Babinski J: Reflexes de defense. Brain 45:149–184, 1922

Basso, A, Lecours AR, Moraschini S, et al: Anatomoclinical correlations of the aphasics as defined through the computerized tomography: exceptions. Brain Lang 26:201–229, 1985

Baxter LR, Phelps ME, Mazziotta JC, et al: Cerebral metabolic rates for glucose in mood disorder: studies with positron emission tomography and fluorodeoxyglucose F18. Arch Gen Psychiatry 42:441–447, 1985

Borden W: Psychological aspects of stroke: patients and family. Ann Intern Med 57:189–194, 1986

Broca P: New finding of aphasia following a lesion of the posterior part of the second and third frontal convolutions. Bulletin de la Societe Anatomique 6:398–407, 1861

Bryden MP: Laterality: Functional Asymmetry in the Intact Brain. New York, Academic Press, 1982

Bunney WE, Garland BL: Selected aspects of amine and receptor hypothesis of affective illness. J Clin Neuropharmacol 1:35–115, 1981

Damasio AR, Geschwind N: Anatomical localization in clinical neuropsychology, in Handbook of Clinical Neurology, Vol 1 (45): Clinical Neuropsychology. Edited by Frederiks JAM. Amsterdam, Elsevier, 1985

de Bonis M, Dellatolas G, Rondot P: Mood disorders in left and right brain damaged patients: comparison between ratings and self-rating on the same adjective mood scale: some methodological problems. Psychopathology 18:286–292, 1985

Denny-Brown D, Meyer JS, Horenstein S: The significance of perceptual rivalry resulting from parietal lesions. Brain 75:434–471, 1952

Dewberry RG, Lipsey JR, Saad K, et al: Lateralized response to cortical injury in the rat: interhemispheric interaction. Behav Neurosci 100:556–562, 1986

Finkelstein S, Benowitz LJ, Baldessarini RG, et al: Mood, vegetative disturbance and dexamethasone suppression test after stroke. Ann Neurol 12:463–468, 1982

Fisher A: Psychiatric considerations of cerebral vascular disease: Am J Cardiol 7:379, 1961

Folstein MF, Maiberger R, McHugh PR: Mood disorder as a specific complication of stroke. J Neurol Neurosurg Psychiatry 41:470–473, 1978

Gainotti G: Reactions catastrophiques et manifestations d'indifference au cours des atteintes cerebrales. Neuropsychologia 7:195–204, 1969

Gainotti G: Emotional behavior and hemispheric side of the lesion. Cortex 8:41–55, 1972

Gainotti G: Laterality of affect: the emotional behavior of right and left brain damaged patients, in Hemisyndromes: Psychobiology, Neurology, Psychiatry. Edited by Myslobodsky M. New York, Academic Press, 1983

Gasparrini WG, Satz P, Heilman KM, et al: Hemispheric asymmetries of affective processing as determined by the Minnesota Multiphasic Personality Inventory. J Neurol Neuosurg Psychiatry 41:470–473, 1978

Goldstein K: Aftereffects of Brain Injuries in War. New York, Grune and Stratton, 1942

Gruzelier JH, Venables PH: Skin conductance response to tones with and without attentional significance in schizophrenics and non-schizophrenic patients. Neuropsychologia 8:119–128, 1973

Gurzelier JH, Venables PH: Bimodality and lateral asymmetry of skin conductance orienting activity in schizophrenics: replication and evidence of lateral asymmetry in patients with depression and disorders of personality. Biol Psychiatry 8:55–73, 1974

Hamilton MA: A rating scale for depression. J Neurol Neurosurg Psychiatry 23:56–62, 1960

Hecaen H, de Ajuriaguerra J, Massonet: Les troubles visuoconstructives par lesion parietoocipitale droit. Encephale 40:122–179, 1951

Hoes MJAJM: Depression and mania, in Handbook of Clinical Neurology, Vol 2: Neurobehavioral Disorders. Edited by Vinken PJ, Bruyn GW. Amsterdam, Elsevier, 1985

Hollister LE: Tricyclic antidepressants. N Engl J Med 200:1106–1109, 1978

Kinsbourne M: The minor cerebral hemisphere as a source of aphasic speech. Arch Neurol 25:202–306, 1971

Kinsbourne M: Eye and head-turning indicates cerebral lateralization. Science 176:539–541; 1972

Levine DN, Mohr JP: Language after bilateral cerebral infarctions: role of the minor hemisphere in speech. Neurology 29:927–938, 1979

Lipsey JR, Robinson RG, Pearlson GD, et al: Mood change following bilateral hemisphere brain injury. Br J Psychiatry 143:266–273, 1983

Lipsey JR, Robinson RG, Pearlson GD, et al: Nortriptyline treatment for post-stroke depression: a double blind study. Lancet 1:297–300, 1984

Meyer JS, Stoica E, Pasco I, et al: Catecholamine concentrations in CSF and plasma of patients with cerebral infarction and hemorrhage. Brain 96:277, 1973

Milner B: Hemispheric specialization: scope and limits, in The Neurosciences: Third Study Program. Edited by Schmitt FO, Worden FG. Cambridge Mass, MIT Press, 1974

Morrison JM, Molliver ME, Grzanna R: Noradrenergic innervation of cerebral cortex: widespread effects of local cortical lesions. Science 205:313–316, 1979

Myslobodsky MS, Horesh N: Bilateral electrodermal activity in depressive patients. Biol Psychology 6:111–222, 1978

Pearlson GD, Robinson RG: Suction lesions of the frontal cerebral cortex in the rat induced asymmetrical behavioral and catecholaminergic responses. Brain Res 218:233–242, 1981

Perria L, Rossadini G, Rossi GF: Determination of side of cerebral dominance with amobarbital. Arch Neurol 4:173–181, 1961

Phelps ME, Mazziotta JC, Gerner RH, et al: Human cerebral glucose metabolism in affective disorders: drug-free states and pharmacological effects. J Cereb Blood Flow Metab 3(51):57–58, 1983

Reis DJ, Ross RD, Gilad G, et al: Reaction of central catecholaminergic neurons to injury: model systems for studying the neurobiology of central regeneration and sprouting, in Neuronal Plasticity. Edited by Cotman CW. New York, Raven Press, 1978

Robinson RG: Differential behavioral and biochemical effects of right and left hemisphere cerebral infarctions in the rat. Science 205:707–710, 1979

Robinson RG, Coyle JT: The differential effect of right vs. left hemisphere cerebral infarction on catecholamines and behavior in the rat. Brain Res 188:63-78, 1980

Robinson RG, Price TR: Post-stroke depressive disorders: a follow-up study of 103 patients. Stroke 13:635–641, 1982

Robinson RG, Shoemaker WJ, Schlumpf M: Time course of changes in catecholamines follows right hemisphere cerebral infarction in the rat. Brain Res 181:202–208, 1980

Robinson RG, Starr LB, Kubos KL, et al: A two year longitudinal study of post-stroke mood disorders: findings during the initial evaluation. Stroke 14:736–714, 1983

Robinson RG, Kubos KL, Starr LB, et al: Mood disorders in stroke patients: importance of location of lesion. Brain 107:81–93, 1984a

Robinson RG, Starr LB, Lipsey JR, et al: A two year longitudinal study of post-stroke mood disorders: dynamic changes in associated variables over the first six months of follow-up. Stroke 15:510–517, 1984b

Robinson RG, Lipsey JR, Bolla-Wilson K, et al: Mood disorders in left-handed stroke patients. Am J Psychiatry 142:1424–1429, 1985

Sackeim HD, Greenburg MS, Weiman AL, et al: Hemispheric asymmetry in the expression of positive and negative emotions: neurologic evidence. Arch Neurol 39:210–218, 1982

Sandel A, Alcorn JD: Individual hemisphericity and maladaptive behavior. J Abnorm Psychol 89:514–517, 1980

Schildkraut JJ: The catecholamine hypothesis of affective disorders: a review of supporting evidence. Am J Psychiatry 122:509, 1965

Sinyor P, Jacques P, Kaloupek DG, et al: Post-stroke depression and lesion location: an attempted replication. Brain 109:537–546, 1986

Starkstein SE, Robinson RG, Price TR: Comparison of cortical and subcortical lesions in the production of post-stroke mood disorders. Brain 110:1045–1059, 1987

Terzian H, Cecotto C: Su un nuovo metodo per la determinazione e lo studio della dominanza emisferica. G Psychiatr Neuropathol 87:889–924, 1959

Toone BK, Cooke E, Lader D: Electrodermal activity in affective disorders and schizophrenia. Psychol Med 11:497–508, 1981

Tsunoda T, Oka M: Lateralization for emotion in the human brain and auditory cerebral dominance. Proc Jpn Acad 52:528–531, 1976

Tucker DM: Lateral brain function, emotion and conceptualization. Psychol Bull 69:19–46, 1981

Vignolo LA, Boccardi E, Caverni L: Unexpected CT-scan findings in global aphasia. Cortex 22:55–69, 1986

Watson RT, Valenstein E, Day AL, et al: The effect of corpus callosum lesions on unilateral neglect in monkey. Neurology 34:812–815, 1984

Wernicke C: Der Aphasiche Symptomenocomplex. Breslau, Max Cohn and Weigart, 1874

Wing JK, Cooper JK, Sartorius N: Measurement and Classification of Psychiatric Symptoms. Cambridge, Cambridge University Press, 1974

Wolf PA, Dawber TR, Thomas HE, et al: Epidemiology of stroke, in Advances in Neurology. Edited by Thompson RA, Green JR. New York, Raven Press, 1977

Zervas NT, Hori H, Nesora M: Reduction of brain dopamine following experimental cerebral ischemia. Nature 247:283, 1974

Zung WWK: A self-rating depression scale. Arch Gen Psychiatry 12:63–70, 1965

Chapter 3

Depressed Mood and Reduced Emotionality after Right-Hemisphere Brain Damage

Arnstein Finset, Ph.D.

Chapter 3

Depressed Mood and Reduced Emotionality after Right-Hemisphere Brain Damage

Depressed mood after stroke and other cerebral damage has most often been associated with left-hemisphere (LH) lesions. Recent research, however, has indicated that the nature and severity of depressive affect may depend both on laterality and caudality of lesions. In this chapter, I will discuss qualitative aspects of depressed mood seen in patients with right-hemisphere (RH) lesions. I will present research on emotional-indifference reactions and on deficient affective processing after RH damage, and I will discuss the possibility of a common underlying mechanism for depressed mood and reduced emotionality in RH lesion patients. Finally, I will describe the clinical implications of these viewpoints.

The most common concepts to describe emotional changes following unilateral brain damage through the 1970s were the *catastrophic reaction* with anxiety and depressive affect supposed to follow LH lesions and *indifference reactions* related to RH lesions (Gainotti 1983).

Goldstein (1939, 1948), who coined the term, saw the catastrophic reaction as the response of the organism to a threatening situation, rather than a specific symptom related to localized brain damage. The immediate pattern of the catastrophic reaction is, according to Goldstein, anxiety; depression occurs more as its prolonged after-effect.

In a frequently cited study, Gainotti (1972) examined the emo-

---

This work was supported in part by grants from the Norwegian Council for Social Science and the Humanities and from the Norwegian Council for Heart and Coronary disease. I thank R. G. Robinson, M. Lezak, Don M. Tucker, and K. Sundet for valuable comments on earlier drafts.

tional behavior of 160 stroke patients, 80 with LH and 80 with RH lesions. Patients were given a standard neuropsychological examination. All verbal expressions during these examinations were transcribed verbatim, and behavior was categorized according to a list of emotional behaviors that was based on existing literature in the field. These emotional behaviors and reactions were classified in three broad categories: catastrophic reactions, depressive moods, and indifference reactions. Gainotti found that five of the eight behaviors classified as indicators of catastrophic reactions were significantly more frequent in the LH lesion group than in the RH lesion group. All five behaviors that indicated indifference reactions were more frequent among RH than LH lesion patients.

The indicators of depressive mood were somewhat more frequent in LH-damaged patients but the increase was not significant.

DEPRESSED MOOD AFTER UNILATERAL BRAIN DAMAGE

Gainotti's findings on depression might be interpreted to suggest that depressive affect after stroke is not specifically related to the location of the lesion. Depression may be thought to occur as a secondary psychogenic reaction to the disability suffered after a stroke. Thus, Robins (1976) studied 18 stroke-disabled patients and 18 non-stroke-disabled patients matched for age and sex with the stroke-disabled patients and with a corresponding degree of disability. The stroke patients were somewhat more markedly depressed than the nonstroke patients, as rated by the Hamilton Rating Scale (Hamilton 1960), but the difference did not reach statistical significance. Robins does not report the laterality of the lesions. He concludes that depression in stroke patients is "a similar phenomenon to that seen in non-brain damaged medically ill patients, i.e., a non-specific affective response to the complex physical and psychological stresses imposed by the illness" (p. 481).

However, if laterality is taken into account, a majority of the studies report depressed mood to be more frequent after LH than RH damage. Gasparrini et al. (1978) found 7 of 16 patients with LH and 0 of 8 RH patients to have elevated scores on the Minnesota Multiphasic Personality Inventory depression subscore. Robinson and colleagues have in several studies found depression more frequent after LH than RH stroke. In one study of 193 stroke patients, Robinson and Price (1982) found that 49 percent of LH patients and only 7 percent of RH patients had a clinically significant depression. Finkelstein et al. (1982) found depression a little more common in RH patients than was reported in the studies just mentioned, but it was still much less common than that reported in LH patients (25 and 69 percent, respectively).

In some studies, however, depressive affect has also been associated with RH damage. Folstein et al. (1977) examined 20 stroke patients and 20 physically impaired orthopedic patients. The stroke patients included 10 LH-damaged and 10 RH-damaged patients. Five of the LH patients, four in the RH group, and only one orthopedic patient were rated as depressed. The depression rating scores (again based on the Hamilton scale) were somewhat higher in the RH group, who also suffered from an overall increase in psychological symptoms, particularly irritability.

In a study of 22 stroke patients, Raymond and Susset (1984) found that depression was unrelated to lesion location, but did find a correlation between lesion location and return of physical functions.

In the head injury literature, changes in emotional behavior is often related to RH damage (Lishman 1979; Damasio 1979). Lishman (1979) suggests that in head injury patients depressive reactions appear to be related to right-frontal and parietal lesions. But the frequent bilateral nature of closed head injuries makes it difficult to interpret possible laterality effects.

Kulesha et al. (1981), who studied patients with systemic lupus erythematosus involving the cerebrum, found a striking incidence of depressive affect when the lesion was in the right hemisphere.

Recently, the incidence and intensity of depressed mood after strokes has also been related to the *caudality* of the lesion.

Robinson and colleagues have extensively studied the effects of caudality of the lesion. In one study comparing LH stroke patients with LH traumatically brain-injured patients, the investigators reported that the increased severity of depression in stroke patients could be explained by intergroup differences in the caudality of the lesion location (Robinson and Szetela 1981).

A second study was conducted using 22 LH and 14 RH lesion patients during the acute poststroke period (Robinson et al. 1983). On several measures of depression, i.e., the Zung Depression Scale (a self-rating scale; Zung 1965), the Hamilton Depression Scale (an interviewer-rated scale; Hamilton 1960), and the Present State Exam (a structured psychiatric interview; Wing et al. 1974), the left anterior lesion group had significantly higher depression scores than either left-posterior or right-anterior lesion patients. In addition, the severity of depression in this group was significantly correlated with the caudality of the lesion (Robinson et al. 1984). However, among the patients with RH lesions, those with right-posterior damage had a significantly higher mean overall depression score than those with right-anterior lesions, and the severity of depression was significantly correlated with the caudality of the lesion location but in the opposite direction than in patients with LH lesions (Robinson et al. 1984).

The importance of the caudality of the lesion was also confirmed in patients with bilateral lesions (Lipsey et al. 1983). In 15 patients with both RH and LH brain injury, the severity of depression was greater in those with left-anterior brain injury than in those with left-posterior damage. This finding was independent of the location of the RH lesion or whether the right or left lesion was more acute.

These data indicate that depression does not occur in all LH lesion patients, but is significantly increased in patients with left-frontal lesions. On the other hand, among patients with RH stroke, depression ratings were significantly higher for patients with RH posterior infarcts than for patients with right-anterior lesions.

In a recent attempted replication of Robinson and collaborators' work, Sinyor et al. (1986) found in their sample of 35 stroke patients no statistically significant relationship between depression and lesion location, although the trend in LH patients was in the same direction as that reported by Robinson and co-workers. In RH patients, a curvilinear relationship appeared, with anterior and posterior lesions associated with high depression scores. Sinyor and co-workers conclude that lesion location may be related to the severity of poststroke depression, but that the nature of the relationship may be more complex than hitherto suggested.

Finset (1982a) studied 40 stroke patients with left hemiplegia. Based on global ratings of depressive affect, he found patients with pure posterior lesions to be significantly more depressed than patients with frontal damage. In a more carefully controlled study, Finset et al. (submitted for publication) applied several measures of depressive affect, including a global rating scale, a revised version of the Norwegian ADI-scale (Havik and Maeland 1984), and relevant items from the CPRS, a psychiatric rating scale developed by British and Swedish researchers (Asberg et al. 1978; von Knorring and Strandman 1978). They found that patients tended to show a significantly more depressed mood if their RH lesions were both posterior and deep, affecting both cortical and subcortical areas in the posterior part of the hemisphere. Curiously, they found patients with pure cortical lesions over the parietal convexity of the hemisphere to have a low incidence of depressed mood.

In summary, studies of depression after stroke and other unilateral brain damage do not produce a clear picture when only the laterality of the lesion is taken into account. However, studies that examine both questions of laterality and caudality of lesion may unmask a pattern that disappears in studies that simply compare right with left lesions. For instance, Robinson et al. (1983) found in an unselected group of 103 acute stroke patients that depression scores of patients with RH lesions were not significantly different from those of patients with LH lesions; however, when caudality of the lesion was taken into account, patients with left-frontal lesions were significantly more depressed than any other group. When only right-left lesion location is taken into account, depression and indifference effects may cancel each other out. The most significant difference between groups emerges when laterality, caudality, and even depth of lesion are taken into account.

This conclusion is well in keeping with current warnings not to overemphasize laterality differences. As Sperry (1982) aptly formulated it in his Nobel lecture: "The left-right dichotomy in cognitive mode is an idea with which it is very easy to run wild. Qualitative shifts in mental control may involve up-down, front-back, or various other organizational changes as well as left-right differences" (p. 1225).

THE NATURE OF RH DEPRESSED MOOD

The inconsistencies in the findings of depressed mood after RH lesion may indicate that different criteria for depressive affect have been used in the respective studies. In their recent review of the literature on emotional changes after unilateral brain damage, Kinsbourne and Bemporad (1984) suggest that the "right posterior hemisphere" depression observed by Robinson and Szetela (1981) and Finset (1982a) may differ qualitatively from "the 'left anterior depression' reported in the majority of the literature" (p. 268).

An obvious problem is also the different criteria for depressed mood applied in the respective studies, ranging from Minnesota Multiphasic Personality Inventory scores via questionnaires to psychiatric rating scales. There are a wide variety of depressive symptoms and many subtypes of depressive reactions, although Beck et al. (1975) observe that the cognitive themes of the depressive are remarkably similar regardless of subtype.

In this chapter, I have deliberately chosen the concepts of *depressed mood* and *depressive affect* rather than the more global word "depression" to denote the specific affect or mood component in depression. A lowering of the mood level, making the patient look sad, most often accompanied by a subjective feeling of being sad, is characteristic of most depressed patients. Whether or not the symptomatology also includes an elaboration of depressed thought content, sleep and appetite disturbances, and other vegetative signs, inner tensions, anxiety, and so forth is not indicated by the terms "depressed mood" and "depressive affect" as I use them.

Although there are no studies to date (to my knowledge) that compare the qualitative aspects of depressive affect of RH versus LH patients, there are some indicators of differences between the two types of depressive reactions.

Finset and Haakonsen (1985), in their study of stroke patients with RH lesions, computed a "depression profile" based on scores from 33 patients on each of 10 Comprehensive Psychiatric Rating Scale (CPRS) items used in their study. They found relatively high scores on those items that measure diffusely depressed mood, whereas depressive thought and especially suicidal thoughts were less frequent. Also, anxiety and inner tension and vegetative signs of depression were uncommon in this sample. Lack of initiative and concentration problems were a little more frequent, but these disturbances may be more directly related to brain damage independent of depressed mood.

A specific complication in interpreting the CPRS items in the RH sample is the lack of insight and denial of illness characteristic of RH patients (Weinstein and Kahn 1955; Gainotti 1972; Finset 1981). Some patients may display a distinctly depressed mood, but will verbally deny that they are depressed. This is in line with the findings of Grafman et al. (1985) that RH patients may look more depressed than they say they are.

In Finset and Haakonsen's (1985) sample a 60-year-old male patient with constructional apraxia, body neglect, and inattention to his own symptoms illustrates this phenomenon. He answered when asked if he felt sad and depressed: "No, I would not say sad or depressed exactly, maybe a little down." Team members all rated him as displaying a depressed mood. He denied experiencing reduced feeling, but his wife reported a marked lack of interest in his grandchildren, for example.

Descriptions given by several authors indicate a somewhat different clinical picture in depressed patients with LH damage. Gainotti (1972) reports significantly more anxiety and other catastrophic reactions in LH than RH patients, and Robinson et al. (1983, 1984) found their depressed LH patients more severely depressed, using conventional psychiatric criteria, than their RH patients.

These indicators of differences in the nature of depressive affect between RH and LH patients are all the more interesting in the light of recent research on psychopathology and cerebral asymmetries. Ever since Flor-Henry's (1969) study on temporal-lobe epilepsies, there has been a growing amount of research investigating the proposed link between RH dysfunction and affective disorders (Tucker 1981; Myslobodsky 1983).

In a frequently cited article, Ross and Rush (1984) conclude that both hemispheres participate in the depressive syndrome, although in different ways. Perris and Monakhov (1979) similarly found that their research confirmed the possible specialized participation of either of the brain hemispheres in the syndromes of depression. More recently, Perris (1986) has suggested that whereas the mood component in depression may be related to RH dysfunctioning, the cognitive content and anxiety components seem to be related to LH functioning. Tucker and Williamson (1984) have suggested that asymmetry effects in psychopathology may be due to the neurochemical laterality of neurotransmitter functioning in the human brain (see also Glick 1983).

To summarize, it seems that the RH-damaged depressed patient is characterized by a generally lowered mood level with little specifically depressive symptomatology and often with a certain degree of inertia and lack of initiative, whereas the depressed LH patient is more severely depressed, with more outspoken symptoms and a higher degree of anxiety. Within the RH group, distinctions should be made between patients with depression in a strict psychiatric sense and patients with a diffusely depressed mood. Indeed, it has been suggested that RH patients with a diffusely depressed mood should not be called depressed. The alternative term "organic inertia" has been suggested (Samuels 1984).

EMOTIONAL INDIFFERENCE AFTER RH DAMAGE

As indicated in the introduction, RH-damaged patients have most often been described in the literature as indifferent rather than depressed. The notion of an indifference reaction in *right* brain-damaged patients was first proposed by Babinski as early as 1914 in his classical paper on denial of illness in left hemiplegia (anosognosia). "I have also observed," says Babinski, "some hemiplegics, who, without ignoring the existence of their paralysis, seem to attach no importance to it, as if it was an insignificant illness" (Babinski 1914, quoted by Critchley 1971).

Hecaen et al. (1951) and Denny-Brown et al. (1952) also describe the indifference reaction of RH patients. Denny-Brown et al. describe a patient whose personality variously described as "indifference" or "placidity" was particularly noticeable. The patient was not apathetic; she maintained a superficial interest in watching what went on around her, but her attitude was entirely passive; she lacked initiative

(p. 468). In the literature, emotional indifference has often been associated with denial of illness.

Some authors relate the indifference reaction to a right-frontal lesion. In discussing the unconcerned "blunt" and "tame" quality of emotional behavior in frontal lobe patients, Damasio suggests that "bilateral or right-frontal damage is probably more conducive to the disturbances than in left-frontal damage" (1979, p. 401), and Kolb and Whishaw (1980) propose that the "pseudo psychopathic" traits described by Blumer and Benson (1975) as indicative of orbito-frontal damage may be more typical in right-sided than in left-sided lesions. Robinson et al. (1984) found right-frontal patients clearly less depressed than both left-frontal and right-posterior stroke patients.

DEPRESSED MOOD AND EMOTIONAL INDIFFERENCE: A POSSIBLE COMMON UNDERLYING MECHANISM?

There are certain interesting parallels between the diffuse RH state of depressed mood and the indifference reaction often proposed as typical of RH patients. The two symptoms are not the same phenomenon. In fact, in Finset's (1982a) study measures of depressed mood and indifference showed a significant negative correlation. But the categories share the traits of lack of initiative and concentration and a characteristic emotional shallowness that might be described as reduced emotionality.

The reduced emotionality seen in many RH patients may be related to a lessened ability to comprehend emotionally charged stimuli. Several studies over the last few years have found indications of such a disability in RH patients. (See reviews by Gainotti 1983; Heilman 1983; and Tucker 1981.) Tucker et al. (1976) found patients with right temporo-parietal lesions to have a reduced capacity to discriminate among nonverbal emotional cues. DeKosky et al. (1980) found RH patients more deficient than LH patients both in discriminating among and generating emotional stimuli. Wechsler (1973) found RH patients to be less effective than LH patients in remembering emotionally charged narrative texts, and Gardner et al. (1975) found RH patients to be inefficient in processing verbal tasks with emotional content.

The diminished capacity to mediate emotionally charged material seen in RH patients has a parallel in studies of normal persons (see review by Moscovitch 1983). In tachistoscopic recognition tasks (Suberi and McKeever 1977; Ley and Bryden 1979), tasks in which films are presented to separate visual fields by means of special contact lenses (Dimond and Farrington 1977), tasks involving dichotic listening (Carmon and Nachson 1973; Safer and Leventhal 1977), and EEG recordings (Harman and Ray 1977), RH superiority for mediation of emotionally charged materials has been found.

Overall, available evidence indicates that a posterior RH lesion may cause a breakdown in the proposed specialized function of that region to decode the emotional meaning of stimuli. This deficiency may make the patient more dependent on verbal explanations provided by oneself or others to give emotional meaning to events in the environment. Such a deficiency could be called emotional or affective agnosia (Finset 1982a).

CLINICAL IMPLICATIONS

Despite certain ambiguities in the research literature on depressed mood after RH brain damage, the following tentative conclusions are warranted at this stage of research.

First, the frequency of depressed mood after RH damage seems to be related to caudality and possibly depth of lesion. Both Robinson and colleagues and Finset and colleagues have found a characteristic lack of depressed mood in patients with anterior lesions, linking the depressive reaction to patients with posterior, possibly deep posterior, lesions.

Secondly, those RH patients who do show a depressed mood will only seldom exhibit a full-fledged depression with depressive thought content and anxiety reactions. This lack of depressive symptomatology is so prominent that some clinicians hesitate to label the RH mood disturbance a depressive reaction at all.

Both these conclusions, the correlation with intrahemispheric location and the differences from other depressive reactions, indicate the organic nature of the depressed mood associated with RH damage. This conception of RH depressed mood has important clinical implications.

If RH depressed mood were to be considered as solely a psychogenic grief reaction brought about as a reaction to disability, a psychotherapeutic approach aiming at an emotional working through of depressive affect would be advised. Moreover, antidepressants would probably be of little use.

The literature on different treatment approaches to depression after stroke or other acquired brain damage is sparse, and studies evaluating such an approach do not seem to exist. Our own clinical experience indicates that RH patients respond poorly to conventional psychotherapy. We have even found that some patients become more depressed when psychotherapy of their depressive affect is attempted.

The view that depressed mood in RH patients has an organic component implies that the patient more or less wrongfully attributes his or her depressive affect to sad experiences in the recent past, most notably to the stroke (or other cerebral insult) and its consequences (for example, pareses). I have suggested that an adequate psychotherapeutic response to RH depressed mood would be a *reattribution* therapy approach (Finset 1982b).

The term "reattribution therapy" is taken from cognitive-behavioral therapy (Meichenbaum 1977; Dweck and Repucci 1973). It implies an effort on the part of the therapist to help the patient correct wrongful conceptions (misattributions) concerning himself or herself. In cases of RH brain damage, an early explanation to the patient that depression is a very common concomitant symptom in persons with this particular lesion may prevent him or her from being too absorbed by depressed thoughts. The cognitive content of therapy would be a reattribution rather than emotional working through and emphasize (and preferably make provisions for) physical and mental activity.

The RH depressed patient's ability to interpret emotionally loaded material is reduced. The patient is vulnerable to pessimistic interpretations. Reattribution therapy may give the patient a cognitive structure to compensate for the loss of ability to interpret emotional stimuli.

Antidepressant drugs may be indicated. Lipsey et al. (1984) administered nortriptyline to stroke patients in a double-blind study. The treated group, including both LH and RH patients, showed significantly better remission than the placebo group. Finset and Drolsum (1983) tested doxepin in an unpublished pilot study with 14 depressed RH patients; they observed that the treated group showed a statistically significantly better remission rate than the placebo group.

CONCLUSION

I have reviewed the literature on depressed mood after RH damage. The findings are far from conclusive. As indicated in the preceding section, further empirical findings or confirmations on this topic will have not only academic value but important clinical implications as well.

The next logical step would be a well-controlled study in which symptoms of depressive affect are measured in both RH and LH patients, as well as in control groups with psychogenic depressions and depressed mood after physical, noncerebral illness. Such a study might elucidate some of the unanswered questions in this field.

REFERENCES

Asberg M, Montgomery C, Perris C, et al: The CPRS: a comprehensive psychopathological rating scale. Acta Psychologica Scandinavica 271:5–28, 1978

Babinski, J: Contribution a l'etude des troubles menteaux dans l'hemiplegie cerebrale (anosognosie). Rev Neurol (Paris) 27:845–847, 1914

Beck AT, Rush AJ, Shaw BF, et al: Cognitive Therapy of Depression. New York, Grune and Stratton, 1975

Blumer D, Benson DF: Personality changes with frontal and temporal lobe lesions, in Psychiatric Aspects of Neurologic Disease. Edited by Benson DF, Blumer D. New York, Grune and Stratton, 1975

Carmon A, Nachson I: Ear asymmetry in perception of emotional non-verbal stimuli. Acta Psychologica 37:351–357, 1973

Critchley M: The Parietal Lobes. New York, Hafner, 1971

Damasio A: The frontal lobes, in Clinical Neuropsychology. Edited by Heilman WM, Valenstein E. New York, Oxford University Press, 1979

DeKosky ST, Heilman KM, Bowers D, et al: Recognition and discrimination of emotional faces and pictures. Brain Lang 9:206–214, 1980

Denny-Brown D, Meyer JS, Horenstein S: The significance of perceptual rivalry resulting from parietal lesions. Brain 75:433–471, 1952

Dimond SJ, Farrington L: Emotional response to films shown to the right or left hemisphere of the brain measured by heart rate. Acta Psychologica 41:255–260, 1977

Dweck CS, Repucci ND: Learned helplessness and reinforcement responsibility in children. Journal of Personality and Social Psychology 25:109–116, 1973

Finkelstein S, Benowitz LI, Baldessarini RJ, et al: Mood, vegetative disturbance and dexamethasone suppression test after stroke. Ann Neurol 12:463–468, 1982

Finset A: Benekting av sykdom og funksjonssvikt ved hemiplegi [Denial of illness and functional losses in hemiplegia]. Journal of the Norwegian Psychological Association 18:407–415, 1981

Finset A: Depressive behavior, outbursts of crying, and emotional indifference in left hemiplegics. Paper presented at the 2nd International Symposium on Models and Techniques of Cognitive Rehabilitation. Indianapolis, IN, March 1982a

Finset A: Cognitive-affective reintegration of function: an approach to the treatment of emotional disorders in the brain damaged. Paper presented at the 2nd International Symposium on Models and Techniques of Cognitive Rehabilitation. Indianapolis, IN, March 1982b

Finset A, Drolsum A: Antidepressant drug therapy for stroke patients with left hemiplegia: results from a medication trial. Unpublished manuscript, 1983

Finset A, Haakonsen M: Depression in patients with right hemisphere CVA. Presented at the 8th European Conference of the International Neuropsychological Society, Copenhagen, Denmark, 15 June 1985

Finset A, Goffeng L, Landro NI, et al: Depressed mood and intra-hemispheric location of lesion in right hemisphere stroke patients. Submitted for publication

Flor-Henry P: Psychosis and temporal lobe epilepsy: a controlled investigation. Epilepsia 10:363–395, 1969

Folstein MF, Maiberger R, McHugh P: Mood disorder as a specific complication of stroke. J Neurol Neurosurg Psychiatry 40:1018–1020, 1977

Gainotti G: Emotional behavior and hemispheric side of lesion. Cortex 8:41–55, 1972

Gainotti G: Laterality of affect: the emotional behavior of right- and left-brain-damaged patients, in Hemisyndromes. Edited by Myslobodsky MS. New York, Academic Press, 1983

Gardner H, Ling PK, Flamm L, et al: Comprehension and appreciation of humorous material following brain damage. Brain 98:399–412, 1975

Gasparrini WG, Satz P, Heilman KM, et al: Hemispheric asymmetries of affective processing as determined by the MMPI. J Neurol Neurosurg Psychiatry 41:470–473, 1978

Glick SD: Cerebral lateralization in the rat and tentative extrapolations in man, in Hemisyndromes. Edited by Myslobodsky MS. New York, Academic Press, 1983

Goldstein K: The Organism. New York, American Book Company, 1939

Goldstein K: Langauge and Language Disturbances. New York, Grune and Stratton, 1948

Grafman J, Weingartner H, Vance S, et al: Persistent abnormal mood changes following penetrating brain wounds. Presented at the 8th European Conference of the International Neuropsychological Society, Copenhagen, Denmark, 13 June 1985

Hamilton M: A rating scale for depression. J Neurol Neurosurg Psychiatry 23:56–62, 1960

Havik O, Maeland OG: ADI-skjemaet (The ADI-Inventory). Journal of the Norwegian Psychological Association 20:70–78, 1983

Hecaen H, de Ajuriaguera J, Massonet J: Les troubles visuoconstructifs par lesions parieto-occipitale droite. Encephale 40:122–179, 1951

Heilman KM, Watson RT, Bowers D: Affective disorders associated with hemispheric disease, in Neuropsychology of Human Emotion. Edited by Heilman KM, Satz P. New York, Guilford Press, 1983

Kinsbourne M, Bemporad B: Lateralization of emotion: a model and the evidence, in The Psychobiology of Affective Development. Edited by Fox N, Davidson RJ. Hillsdale, NJ, Erlbaum, 1984

Kolb B, Whishaw IQ: Fundamentals in Human Neuropsychology. San Francisco, Freeman, 1980

Kulesha D, Moldofsky H, Urowitz M, et al: Brain scan lateralization and psychiatric symptoms in systemic lupus erythematosus. Biol Psychiatry 16:407–412, 1981

Ley RG, Bryden MP: Hemispheric differences in processing emotions and faces. Brain Lang 7:127–138, 1979

Lipsey JR, Robinson RG, Pearlson GD, et al: Mood change following bilateral hemisphere brain injury. Br J Psychiatry 143:266–273, 1983

Lipsey JR, Robinson RG, Pearlson GD, et al: Nortriptyline treatment of post-stroke depressions: a double blind treatment trial. Lancet 1:297–300, 1984

Lishman WA: Organic Psychiatry. London, MacMillan, 1979

Meichenbaum D: Cognitive behavior modification: an integrative approach. New York, Plenum, 1977

Moscovitch M: The linguistic and emotional functions of the normal right hemisphere, in Cognitive Processing in the Right Hemisphere. New York, Academic Press, 1983

Myslobodsky MS: Introduction, in Hemisyndromes. Edited by Myslobodsky MS. New York, Academic Press, 1983

Perris C: Personal communication, 1986

Perris C, Monakhov K: Depressive symptomatology and systemic structural analysis of the EEG, in Hemisphere Asymmetries of Function in Psychopathology. Edited by Gruzelier J, Flor-Henry P. Amsterdam, Elsevier, 1979

Raymond P, Susset V: Depression in stroke: further evidence for an organic etiology. Arch Phys Med Rehabil 65:630, 1984 (abstract)

Robins AH: Are stroke patients more depressed than other disabled subjects? J Chronic Diseases 29:479–482, 1976

Robinson RG, Szetela B: Mood changes following left hemisphere brain injury. Ann Neurol 9:447–453, 1981

Robinson RG, Price TR: Post stroke depressive disorders: a follow-up study of 103 outpatients. Stroke 13:635–641, 1982

Robinson RG, Kubos KL, Starr LB, et al: Mood changes in stroke patients: relationships to lesion location. Compr Psychiatry 24:555–556, 1983

Robinson RG, Kubos KL, Starr LB, et al: Mood disorder in stroke patients: importance of location of lesion. Brain 107:81–93, 1984

Ross ED, Rush AJ: Diagnosis and neuroanatomical correlates of depression in brain damaged patients. Arch Gen Psychiatry 18:1344–1354, 1981

Safer MA, Leventhal H: Ear differences in evaluating emotional tones of voice and verbal content. J Exp Psychol [Hum Percept] 3:75–82, 1977

Samuels J: Psychopharmacology and treatment. Presented at the 4th International Symposium on Models and Techniques of Cognitive Rehabilitation. Indianapolis, IN, April 4, 1984

Sinyor D, Jacques P, Kaloupek RG, et al: Post stroke depression and lesion location. Brain 109:537–546, 1986

Sperry R: Some effects of disconnecting the cerebral hemispheres. Science 217:1223–1226, 1982

Suberi M, McKeever WF: Differential right hemispheric memory storage of emotional and non-emotional faces. Neuropsychologia 15:757–768, 1977

Tucker DM: Lateral brain function, emotion and conceptualization. Psychol Bull 89:19–49, 1981

Tucker DM, Williamson P: Asymmetric neural control systems in human self regulation. Psychol Rev 91:185–215, 1984

Tucker DM, Watson RT, Heilman KM: Affective discrimination and evocation in patients with right parietal disease. Neurology 27:947–950, 1977

von Knorring L, Strandman E: A comparison between "Cronholm-Ottosson" depression rating scale and variables concerned with depressive symptomatology, in "The Comprehensive Psychiatric Rating Scale—CPRS." Acta Psychologica Scandinavica 271:45–52, 1978

Wechsler A: The effects of organic brain disease on recall of emotionally charged versus neutral narrative. Neurology 23:130–135, 1973

Weinstein EA, Kahn RL: Denial of Illness. Springfield, IL, 1955

Wing JK, Cooper JE, Sartorius N: Measurement and classification of psychiatric symptoms, in Instruction Manual for the PSE. London, Cambridge University Press, 1974

Zung, WWK: A self-rating depression scale. Arch Gen Psychiatry 12:63–70, 1965

Chapter 4

Regional Brain Dysfunction in Depression

Bruce E. Wexler, M.D.

Chapter 4

Regional Brain Dysfunction in Depression

This volume deals with cerebral involvement in normal and depressed affects. Under this heading we are considering such topics as hemisphere specialization, regional brain function, and laterality of facial movement. Why should these topics interest mental health researchers? How are they relevant to psychiatric disorders? The clearer we can be in answering these questions, the better use we can make of information in these areas in studying and thinking about psychiatric illness. After a brief comment on these questions I will review three sets of studies of regional brain function in depressed patients, with two goals in mind: to describe different research methods and approaches and to describe the range of brain dysfunctions reported in depression. Along the way I will also briefly discuss differences in regional brain dysfunction between schizophrenic and depressed patients and among possible subtypes of depressed patients.

THE RELEVANCE TO DEPRESSION OF CEREBRAL INVOLVEMENT IN NORMAL AFFECT

Depressed patients are heterogeneous with respect to age of onset, natural course, the presence or absence of manic periods, and response to pharmacologic agents. Current research efforts attempt to define distinct clinical syndromes within this mixed group on the basis of distinctive symptom clusters or abnormalities of brain function. If the experience of other branches of medicine is any guide, then the success of these efforts depends on discovering principles of normal brain function. For, as described by Foucault (1973), in other branches of medicine the power of symptom-based nosologies and the availability of physiological tests of diagnostic value both increased only when they were based on an understanding of the normal function of the organ system involved in the disease process. If so, the central problem for psychiatric research today is to develop a model for normal brain physiology on which to base studies of pathophysiological processes. Normative work on the brain basis of affect is important for psychiatric research; it represents an effort to describe and assess aspects of the normal physiology of emotional experience. On it can be based a systematic investigation of pathophysiological aspects of emotional response in psychiatric populations.

The next three sections will describe some studies of regional brain dysfunction in depression. I will then consider further the contribution that studies of depressed patients might make to a general understanding of the normal physiology of emotion, as well as whether studies of mood disorders in stroke patients and studies of emotional response in healthy individuals help organize the findings in depressed patients.

PET STUDIES OF DEPRESSED PATIENTS

The first two studies used positron emission tomography (PET scanning) to measure glucose use in specific brain regions of depressed patients. The assumption is that areas with increased or decreased metabolic activity are in some way dysfunctional (areas with normal metabolic rates might also be dysfunctional).

Buchsbaum et al. (1984) studied 11 depressed patients, 16 schizophrenics, and 19 controls. Of the 11 depressed patients, 10 were bipolar and 1 was unipolar; all were currently depressed; 7 were men and 4 were women; and all had been off medication for at least 2 weeks. The experimental method was as follows. Subjects were seated in a darkened, acoustically isolated room with i.v. lines in both arms and the left arm wrapped in a hot pack to arterialize the venous blood. Five minutes before isotope injection they were asked to close their eyes and keep them closed for the next 35 or 40 minutes. Immediately after isotope injection a series of electric shocks varying in intensity from barely perceptible to unpleasant was administered to the right forearm, one per second for a period of 25 minutes. After this a series of scans was performed over a 60-minute period. The group of depressed patients (essentially bipolars) differed significantly from controls in one respect only: they failed to show the normal gradient of decline in metabolic activity from anterior to posterior portions of the brain. This relative "hypofrontality" was also seen in the schizophrenic patients. The depressed patients actually showed insignificantly greater activity than the controls in all regions. They did not show an absolute decrease in frontal activity but rather a decrease in the ratio of frontal to posterior activity. If we were to pick one feature that was abnormal, it was an increase in posterior activity. The balance between frontal and posterior activity had been altered.

The second PET study (Baxter et al. 1985) examined 11 unipolar and 5 bipolar depressed patients and 9 controls. There were 9 men and 7 women among the patients. All were depressed and all had been off medication for at least 1 week. The procedure differed from that of the first study in that subjects kept their eyes open, there was low ambient room noise and light, and no electrical shock or other specific stimulation was delivered. Bipolar depressed patients had significantly lower overall metabolic rates than controls or unipolars. This is in direct contrast to the previous study, in which bipolars showed greater activity than controls in all regions. Region-by-region analyses demonstrated lower activity in bipolars than controls bilaterally in the frontal lobes, caudate, and thalamus and lower activity than unipolars bilaterally in frontal, temporal, occipital, and parietal lobes as well as in the cingulate, caudate, and thalamus. Unipolars as a group showed a bilateral decrease in activity in each caudate compared to activity in the rest of the same hemisphere. Further analyses have revealed that the caudate/hemisphere difference between unipolar and bipolar patients is greatest when activity in the caudate is compared to activity in the anterior prefrontal cortex (Schwartz et al., in press). Of the 11 unipolars, 3 showed a marked decrease in the left frontal activity that clearly differentiated them from all controls, other psychiatric patients, and neurological patients PET-scanned by this research group. Neither unipolar nor bipolar patients differed from normal controls in the ratio of their anterior to posterior activity.

In summary, in one study bipolar patients showed a generalized increase in metabolic activity and a loss of the normal anterior/posterior gradient. In the next study neither of these observations were confirmed: instead, bipolars showed a generalized decrease in metabolic activity and did not differ from normal controls with regard to the anterior/posterior gradient. The most likely explanation is that in one study subjects were deprived of auditory and visual input but presented with a series of electrical shocks to the arm, while none of these conditions existed in the other study. It is known that changes in experimental conditions less significant than these can lead to large changes in the patterns of regional metabolic activity. (With this in mind I must note that special and unusual conditions are unavoidable concomitants of all PET studies.) In addition to these differences between bipolar patients and normal controls, it appears that at least in some conditions bipolars show less metabolic activity than unipolars in essentially all brain regions, that unipolars as a group may have increased activity in prefrontal areas, and that a subgroup of unipolars may have a specific decrease in left frontal activity. In conclusion: 1) differences in regional metabolic activity between normal controls and depressed patients are task dependent; 2) they can implicate multiple areas in both hemispheres; and 3) differences among subgroups of patients indicate the pathophysiological heterogeneity of affective disorders.

EEG STUDIES OF DEPRESSED PATIENTS

The next two studies used scalp electroencephalogram (EEG) recording to assess regional brain function in depressed patients (d'Elia and Perris 1973; Perris 1975). These two articles were selected because the association between the EEG measures and clinical condition is more convincingly demonstrated than usual by virtue of the facts that the EEG findings 1) are correlated with severity of symptoms, 2) change with clinical recovery, and 3) are observed a second time in a replication study. In both of these studies two measures were extracted from resting EEG for each hemisphere: the mean integrated amplitude (MIA) for 15 20-second blocks, and the within-patient variance (WPV) of the 15 MIA values. Recordings from bilateral bipolar centro-occipital leads (C3-01, C4-02) were used to calculate the MIA. In the second study the amplitude of the visual averaged evoked response (AER) was also recorded, using two symmetrical pairs of electrodes applied over occipital regions. Eighteen psychotically depressed inpatients (5 men, 13 women) participated in the first study. For 6 it was the first episode of illness. The other 12 had had two to seven previous episodes, all without mania. Patients were first tested shortly after admission and again after a series of either electroconvulsive or chemical-convulsive treatments. In the second study 51 psychotically depressed inpatients (18 men, 33 women; mean age 48 years) were tested; 28 unipolar, 4 bipolar, and 19 unspecified. The patients were tested once only, shortly after admission and before being treated. The depth of depression was assessed in both studies with the Cronholm-Ottossen Rating Scale for Depression.

In both studies the MIA over the left hemisphere was less than that over the right shortly after admission, and the degree of this asymmetry was significantly correlated with the severity of depression. With treatment and recovery the MIA over both hemispheres increased, but that over the left increased more, so as to equal that over the right. In both studies the WPV over the left hemisphere was significantly less than that over the right shortly after admission.

Again the degree of this asymmetry was significantly correlated with the severity of depression, and again the asymmetry was eliminated with treatment and recovery. Results with the AER were similar; the amplitude on the left was less than that on the right, and the degree of this asymmetry was significantly correlated with the degree of depression.

In summary, EEG activity over both hemispheres changes with recovery from depression. These changes are much more pronounced over the left than over the right hemisphere and the degree of this asymmetry correlates with the severity of the depression. The more depressed an individual is, the greater the change over the left hemisphere relative to that over the right. Although patients were not selected according to diagnostic subtype, 85 to 90 percent of subjects in each study were unipolars.

It is not known what aspects or dimensions of the functional organization of the brain are reflected in either PET studies or scalp electrical recordings. These uncertainties can be illustrated by analogy with fuel consumption and electrical activity in an automobile. In a car a variety of functional changes can result in similar levels of fuel consumption. A total lack of fuel use is consistent with mechanical failure, but could also result from a sick or vacationing driver who never starts the car. Increased fuel consumption could be found in a high-performance sports car, a poorly tuned old clunker, or an ordinary car moving at normal speed with an emergency brake on. A change in electrical patterns could be due to the use of windshield wipers or defrosters, the activation by loss of oil of an indicator light, or use of the audio system. It is clear that the time periods of analysis in the EEG and PET studies differ dramatically from one another. The PET studies evaluated the cumulative effects of an hour of brain metabolic activity on regional glucose use. The EEG studies evaluated the variability of scalp electrical activity from one 15-second epoch to the next. These differences suggest that the two measures assess different aspects of function.

Nevertheless, two general statements can be made. First, both PET and EEG data indicate extensive and bilateral changes in brain function in depressed patients. Second, both studies raise the possibility of a predominant left-hemisphere dysfunction in unipolar depression. Baxter et al. (1985) found that a subgroup of unipolars had striking deficits in left-frontal activity. D'Elia and Perris (1973) found predominantly left-hemisphere EEG changes in centro-occipital and occipital leads.

PERCEPTUAL ASYMMETRY STUDIES
OF DEPRESSED PATIENTS

The next studies to be described were conducted by my colleagues and myself and examined perceptual asymmetry in depressed patients. Perceptual asymmetry refers to the fact that healthy individuals with intact brains more readily identify stimuli presented in the sensory field opposite the hemisphere specialized for their processing. For example, in most right-handed individuals the left hemisphere is specialized for language function. Consequently, words presented briefly in the right visual field are more accurately and more quickly perceived than words flashed in the left visual field. Such perceptual asymmetry is thought to result from a combination of structural and activational factors. Structurally, the information from stimuli presented in the left sensory field is processed first in the right hemisphere and then transferred via the corpus callosum to the left hemisphere. This input pathway might be less efficient than the pathway directly from the right sensory field to the left hemisphere. In addition, stimulus-specific activation of specialized language association areas in the left hemisphere appears also to activate frontal attentional fields in the left hemisphere and thereby to facilitate processing of sensory information in the right sensory field. The magnitude of perceptual asymmetry reflects the net effect of the functional state of the components along the two input paths, and the degree of activation of the specialized hemisphere. In this paradigm test stimuli serve as probes that are presented selectively to each hemisphere and then follow known neural pathways to a common specialized final processing area.

The three studies used dichotic listening tests to assess perceptual asymmetry. In dichotic tests different stimuli are presented simultaneously one to each ear. Studies in split-brain patients indicate that when the degree of temporal and auditory spectral overlap is sufficient, information from each ear is processed initially only by the opposite hemisphere, and the situation is essentially the same as with single-visual-field presentation (Milner et al. 1968; Sparks and Geschwind 1968; Zaidel 1976; Springer et al. 1978). In our particular dichotic tests the overlap between members of each stimulus pair is so great that the two stimuli fuse into a single auditory percept and subjects only hear one member of each dichotic pair. A laterality score is based on the number of times subjects hear the word presented to their right as compared to their left ears.

In the first study test stimuli were pairs of nonsense syllables beginning and ending with letter "a"—"aba," "ada," etc. (Wexler and Heninger 1979). Twenty-six actively psychotic inpatients were tested weekly throughout hospitalization; 12 met research diagnostic criteria for depression, 8 for schizophrenia, and 6 for schizoaffective disorder. Nine of the depressed patients were unipolar. As patients recovered, the right-ear advantage became more marked, while with clinical deterioration it diminished (e.g., Figure 1). Ratings of overall illness, depressed mood, and thought disorder were all lower when laterality was greater. Findings were similar for depressed, schizophrenic, and schizoaffective patients.

In the second study 19 depressed and 7 schizophrenic inpatients were given two dichotic tests twice each, first when acutely symptomatic and again after clinical improvement (Wexler 1986b). One test was the same nonsense-syllables test that was used in the first study. Stimuli in the second test were pairs of single-syllable words differing from one another only in the initial consonant. There were six distinguishing consonants, and these were the same as the six that made up the nonsense syllables in the first test. The right-ear advantage on the nonsense test increased with recovery, as had been noted in the first study. The right-ear advantage on the word test, however, decreased with recovery. Again, findings were similar in the depressed and the schizophrenic subgroups.

In the third study 41 patients were given both dichotic tests shortly after admission. Subgroups of those 41 patients took the tests again after clinical improvement. Once more asymmetry on the nonsense test was found to increase with recovery, while asymmetry on the word test decreased. Moreover, when the 41 patients were divided

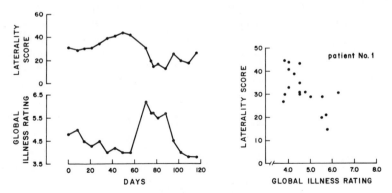

Figure 1. Changes in the magnitude of the right-ear advantage on a dichotic nonsense-syllables test with changes in clinical condition in a 36-year-old depressed woman

into two groups based on laterality scores upon admission, these groups proved to differ symptomatically. The group with greater initial lateral asymmetry on the word test and lower initial laterality on the nonsense test had higher scores on the withdrawal-retardation factor of the Brief Psychiatric Rate Scale. There were equal numbers of both depressed and schizophrenic patients in the two laterality-defined subgroups.

Generalized dysfunction of the left or right hemisphere, or a change in information flow between the hemispheres, might all similarly affect laterality on the word and nonsense tests. Finding opposite changes in asymmetry on the two tests in psychosis then suggests a more specific and limited alteration in brain function. Hypotheses about the nature of this brain dysfunction can be generated by considering the neural processes associated with perceptual asymmetry that were described above. One hypotheses, discussed more fully elsewhere (Wexler 1986b), is based on the role of stimulus-specific activation of the left hemisphere's specialized verbal processing areas and, by extension, activation of left-frontal attention centers, in contributing to the right-ear advantage on language-related dichotic tests. If this activation is altered in depression, laterality would also change. An increase in the right-ear advantage with word stimuli and a decrease with nonsense stimuli would be consistent with increased activation of left-hemisphere language-specialized areas in response to words and decreased activation in response to the nonsense syllables. A unitary explanation of change on both tests can be provided by a two-part hypothesis: 1) normally the functional system of the brain that processes auditory information as meaningful and that which processes it as nonsense are in a mutually inhibitory balance, and 2) in some cases of psychosis this balance shifts in favor of the system that processes information as meaningful (Wexler 1986b). Such a shift would lead to greater left-hemisphere activation in response to words (and an associated increase in the right-ear advantage), and lessened left-hemisphere activation in response to nonsense (and decreased right-ear advantage).

SUMMARY OF EXPERIMENTAL MEASURES

Three different approaches for assessing regional brain function in depressed patients have been described (Table 1). The first, PET scanning, allows highly localized assessment of metabolic activity but at least at present has very coarse temporal resolution. The second, scalp EEG recording, allows very fine time resolution but less precise anatomic localization. The third approach, measuring perceptual asymmetry, allows subtle assessment of brain function in terms that bridge neural and psychological processes. It is, however, poor in anatomic resolution and intermediate in resolution over time.

SUMMARY OF EXPERIMENTAL FINDINGS

When viewed together, these methods demonstrate a variety of brain dysfunctions in depression. Metabolic activity is altered in multiple areas in both hemispheres. Under certain experimental conditions the normal anterior-posterior activity gradient is lost; under other conditions, some patients show a striking diminution of left-prefrontal activity. EEG amplitude and amplitude variability appear to be decreased over both centro-occipital and occipital regions in both hemispheres, although the change is greater over the left. In fact the degree of asymmetry of this change is itself highly correlated with severity of depressive symptoms. Changes in perceptual asymmetry on language-related dichotic listening tests suggest a change in depression in left-hemisphere language-processing systems such that there is abnormal activation of the system that processes auditory verbal information as meaningful. To the degree to which the data from these three sets of studies point to lateralized dysfunction in depression, they indicate primarily left-hemisphere dysfunction. As little as a year ago it was nearly an axiom that schizophrenia was associated with left-hemisphere dysfunction and depression with right-hemisphere dysfunction. The appeals of dichotomous thinking, and of easy mapping of clinical or psychological topographies on brain anatomy, are both powerful and misleading.

Studies with each of the three methods found abnormalities in the interrelation of experimental variables. There is a loss of the normal anterior/posterior gradient in metabolic activity, a change in the ratio

Table 1. Comparison of Experimental Measures

PET Scans
    Good anatomic resolution
    Poor time and questionable functional resolutions

EEG
    Good time resolution
    Moderate anatomic resolution
    Limited functional resolution

Perceptual Asymmetry
    Good functional resolution
    Poor time and anatomic resolutions

---

of left-to-right-hemisphere EEG amplitude, and opposite changes in the magnitude of the right-ear advantage on two highly similar dichotic listening tests. Such results are troubling if the goal is to find a localized deficit associated with depression, for it is not clear whether it is the anterior or posterior region, the right or left hemisphere, or the first or second dichotic test that is abnormal. But if the relationships among different brain regions and among different regional brain functions are the object of study, these results become more satisfying and even somewhat consistent. Studies in depression with PET, EEG, and perceptual asymmetry measures all report changes in relationships between different regions or functions. I have suggested elsewhere that those brain processes that integrate different brain regions (and in so doing also affect the functions that these regions subsume) are the neural correlates of emotion (Wexler 1986a). From this perspective, the alterations in brain function associated with affective disorders would be expected to change the functional relationships among different brain regions.

Both PET data and perceptual asymmetry data demonstrate differences between subgroups of depressed patients and thereby contribute to growing documentation of the pathophysiological heterogeneity of the clinical diagnostic category known as depression. Unipolars differed from bipolars in metabolic activity in almost all brain regions and a subset of unipolars showed specific left-prefrontal changes. Some depressed patients showed the general changes in perceptual asymmetry on the two dichotic tests, while others did not.

Comparisons between schizophrenic and depressed patients are particularly interesting. One PET study found that both schizophrenic and depressed patients differed from controls in the same way, loss of the anterior-posterior gradient, and did not differ from each other. The perceptual asymmetry studies found that the general group changes in asymmetry were the same in both depressed and schizophrenic groups, that the relationship between symptoms and laterality cut across diagnosis, and that subgroups of patients defined on the basis of laterality scores differed in symptom profile but not in diagnostic composition. Buchsbaum et al. (1984), in discussing the fact that both their depressed and schizophrenic patients failed to show the normal posterior gradient in metabolic activity, mentioned a number of other studies that found similar biological changes in schizophrenia and depression, and they suggested that such similarities might be consistent with Meltzer's suggestion that schizophrenic and depressed patients have in common the brain changes that characterize psychosis (Meltzer 1982). Psychosis, in this view, is a unitary, final, common pathophysiological state. But the evidence I have reviewed of pathophysiological heterogeneity within the general diagnostic category of depression suggests another explanation for the overlap between schizophrenic and depressed patients. Differences in brain dysfunction among patients with the same clinical diagnosis and similarities in brain dysfunction among patients with different clinical diagnoses together demonstrate that the fit between current symptom-based diagnostic schemes and pathological processes of the brain is not tight. When the current system-based topography is superimposed on a topography based on regional brain dysfunctions, the two nosologies do not line up with neatly corresponding categories. Some brain dysfunctions would be represented in more than one clinical category (Figure 2).

One goal of this volume is to appraise the extent to which the normal physiology of emotional response and alterations of mood in stroke patients inform and are informed by studies of depressed patients. Such juxtapositions are, based on the current state of knowledge, constrained by three factors. First, depression (the diagnosis or diagnoses) is probably more than, and different from, the emotion of sadness that has been the object of study in normal subjects. Second, studies of depressed and neurological patients have not used the experimental measures and paradigms employed in studies of normal subjects. Third, conceptual understanding of the normal physiology of emotion, and of the general pathophysiology of depression, are insufficient to bridge the gaps between findings that result from studies with procedural differences and those that arise from differences between subject groups that are not related primarily to emotion (e.g., personality characteristics, other physiological aspects of psychotic illnesses).

These obstacles might be overcome, and the anticipated rewards of comparing studies in these different subject groups realized, if

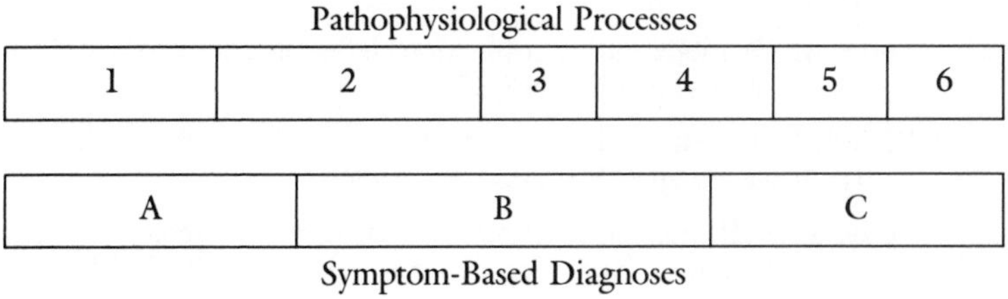

Pathophysiological Processes

1	2	3	4	5	6

A	B	C

Symptom-Based Diagnoses

Figure 2. Possible relationship of pathophysiological processes to symptom-based diagnoses

successive studies of normal, neurological, and psychiatric populations each consider the others' findings and methods. Such an iterative process would facilitate comparison of studies by decreasing methodological differences and begin to fill the space between these groups of studies with a model of the basic physiology of emotion.

REFERENCES

Baxter LR, Phelps ME, Mazziotta JC, et al: Cerebral metabolic rates for glucose in mood disorders. Arch Gen Psychiatry 42:441–447, 1985

Buchsbaum MS, DeLisi LE, Holcomb HH, et al: Anteroposterior gradients in cerebral glucose use in schizophrenia and affective disorders. Arch Gen Psychiatry 41:1159–1166, 1984

d'Elia G, Perris C: Cerebral function dominance and depression. Acta Psychiatr Scand 49:191–197, 1973

Foucault M: The Birth of the Clinic. New York, Pantheon Books, 1973

Meltzer HY: What is schizophrenia? Schizophr Bull 8:433–434, 1982

Milner B, Taylor L, Sperry RW: Lateralized suppression of dichotically presented digits after commissural section in man. Science 161:184–186, 1968

Perris C: EEG techniques in the measurement of the severity of depressive syndromes. Neuropsychobiology 1:16–25, 1975

Schwartz JM, Baxter LR, Mazziotta JC, et al: The differential diagnosis of depression: relevance of positron emission tomography (PET) studies of cerebral glucose metabolism to the bipolar-unipolar dichotomy. J Am Med Assoc (in press)

Sparks R, Geschwind, N: Dichotic listening in men after section of neocortical commissures. Cortex 4:3–16, 1968

Springer SP, Sidtis J, Wilson D, et al: Left ear performance in dichotic listening following commissurotomy. Neuropsychologia 16:305–312, 1978

Wexler BE: A model of brain function: its implications for psychiatric research. Br J Psychiatry 148:357–362, 1986a

Wexler BE: Alterations in cerebral laterality during acute psychotic illness. II. Br J Psychiatry 149:202–209, 1986b

Wexler BE, Heninger GR: Alterations in cerebral laterality during acute psychotic illness. Arch Gen Psychiatry 36:278–288, 1979

Zaidel E: Language, dichotic listening and the disconnected hemispheres, in Conference on Human Brain Function. Edited by Walter DO, Rogers L, Finzi-Fried JM. Los Angeles, BRI Publications Office, 1976

Chapter 5

Cortical Activation in Psychiatric Disorder

Frank B. Wood, Ph.D.
Lynn Flowers, M.A.

Chapter 5

Cortical Activation in Psychiatric Disorder

There is intrinsic appeal to the concept that disorders of human mental or behavioral function might be successfully studied by measuring of localized brain activity. After all, since the brain is the organ and the final common pathway of behavior, disorders of behavior must at least be observable as alterations in brain activity. Indeed, it is widely hoped that the disorders of brain activity, so measured, would be simpler and somehow more "basic" or "fundamental" than their behavioral manifestations have proven to be. In the same way that the genotype is usually more precisely definable than the phenotype in hereditary disease, so it is expected that the "neurotype" will be more precise, less variable, and so more informative than the "behaviorotype" in brain-based diseases or disorders of behavior.

For all its face validity, this expectation that psychiatric disorder will be clarified and better understood when its brain activity concomitants are described is still little more than an assumption. As such, it could benefit from methodological scrutiny. Accordingly, we first consider some of the methodological issues that surround this research paradigm. Only then will it be appropriate to consider our own findings and their relation to the emerging literature.

METHODOLOGICAL ISSUES

Use of a Relevant Activation Task During Measurements of Regional Metabolic Activity or Blood Flow

Depending on the particular technique employed, the measurements will constitute summations of inferred neuronal activity over time periods ranging from a few minutes (in measures of blood flow

Research described in this chapter was supported by U.S. Public Health Service grant no. MH 39599-03.

or oxygen consumption) to perhaps 40 minutes (in measures of local glucose use). Despite this range, it is usually possible to design a behavioral task to be carried out during the flow or metabolic measurements. The use of such a task has practical as well as theoretical advantages. Theoretically, it allows exploration of the state-trait distinction. The assumption underlying this distinction is that state differences are at least part of the psychiatric disorder. This implies that, within a given disorder, various states may differ in their degree of abnormality. Failure to engage subjects in a task that induces a sufficiently pathological state may, therefore, result in a failure to observe abnormalities of brain activity. To be sure, trait differences may be large enough to "swamp" any state differences, but even so—unless the differences are interpreted in reference to clinically or behaviorally significant states—their generality will be unclear, as will their power to explain the disorder in question. An extreme example is the phobic patient whose abnormality is apparent only in the presence of the feared stimulus; but even the relatively chronic state of schizophrenia has periodic exacerbations that may be related to the stimulus context (or its arousal properties).

A related theoretical issue involves the specificity of the task or the state it induces. Most specific psychiatric symptoms or states occur in more than one disorder. Hallucinations, for example, accompany some cases of affective disorder—they are not uniquely schizophrenic symptoms. Induction of a certain behavioral or cognitive state in one type of patient should, therefore, be compared to its induction in other psychopathologies as well as in normality. In this way two major alternative explanations for psychopathology can be differentiated. Either 1) the single behavioral state (hallucination, in our example) has the same brain activity concomitants in whatever form of psychopathological disorder, or 2) different brain states accompany the same behavioral state in different psychopathologies. Either case would be instructive, but neither case can be established unless multiple psychiatric syndromes are investigated by the same methods. Note that there is a third possibility—that of multiple brain states accompanying a single behavioral state within, instead of between, psychopathological syndromes. That is the familiar subtyping notion, except that in this case the subtypes are inferred brain states, not distinguishable at the behavioral level.

There are also practical advantages to using an activation task. These have chiefly to do with the possibility of observing differences in task performance that correlate with differences in brain activation. For example, accuracy of task performance can be correlated with degree of activation of a brain region that is thought to be involved in the execution of the task. This provides an additional explanation of that brain activity variance—an explanation that would not be available if a task were not used. This approach has a major pitfall, however: if differences in task performance (accuracy, for example) are correlated with differences in brain activity, it will still not be possible, readily or easily, to conclude that the task differences actually caused the brain activity differences. A useful strategy is to explore the behavioral domain with other tests of behavioral abilities that relate to the task used. For example, if the task involves an intellectually demanding cognitive operation, then other tests of intelligence or cognitive power should also be given. If these also correlate with the brain activity measurements made during one particular cognitive task, then the specificity of that particular task for generating a certain pattern of brain activity is called into question. This is not to invalidate the approach; indeed, only by systematic explorations of this domain will a network of relationships be found that can clarify the brain-behavior mechanisms at stake.

Variance as a Dependent Measure in Its Own Right

Variances often correlate with means in this line of research (Wood 1982). Metabolic activity measurements are not unlike a variety of physiological measurements in this regard. In particular, there is a tendency for mean metabolic activity measurements at a given site, across subjects, to show increases in variance as the group mean increases. This is partly because there is a physiological floor below which the glucose or flow values do not descend unless there is essentially a widespread necrosis at the site in question. The usual range of values is closer to the physiological floor than to the physiological ceiling, so it is highly informative if there is a correlation across subjects between means and variances at different brain sites. When accompanied by a high variance, a high mean indicates that only some, certainly not all, subjects are showing the high value. The contrasting situation, where a higher mean is accompanied by lower variance, indicates the converse—that the high mean is more generally characteristic of the group than the low mean is. Variance thus constitutes a direct measure of the extent to which a group is in a state of behavioral and neurological constraint. Low variance indicates a uniform constraint upon the group; high variance indicates a lack of constraint.

Relation of Individual Differences to Diagnostic Categories

Psychopathology is often thought of as an instance of normal variation. In this view, based on the premise that individual differences are essentially normal phenomena, a psychopathological disorder represents an extreme case that is, by that definition, relatively uniform. When patterns of brain activity are sought as the defining or at least the clarifying measures for the diagnostic criteria being studied, then it follows that these patterns should be even less variable than the behavioral manifestations.

What if brain activity differences are greater in a psychopathological disorder—greater, that is, than those found among normals, and greater also than the behavioral differences within that disorder? Whether that is the case, is a simple empirical question. If it is, then only behavior, not brain, may be the final common pathway in psychopathology.

If behavior instead of brain is the only final common pathway for a particular psychopathology, then brain states are not thereby rendered less important. There are at least two rather different possibilities for the role of brain states in such an eventuality. The first is the most extreme: that the behavioral abnormality precedes the brain abnormality, so that only prolonged maintenance of the behavioral state results in actual changes of brain organization. The mechanism of such change could be a learned reorganization of brain activity—a form of habituation to the chronic behavioral state. An example might be a progressive social withdrawal that was "driven" by purely behavioral factors, but which led to a pattern of brain organization and activity that involved reduced scanning of the external environment. Alternatively, the altered behavioral state could directly induce a change in brain structure itself. A familiar case in point is the possibility that prolonged stress or arousal may actually modify the structural properties of the brain and its vasculature, with subsequent need to compensate for the altered function that is thereby induced (Kellner et al. 1983; Jensen et al. 1983).

The other possibility is that brain changes temporally precede behavioral changes in psychopathology. This of course begs the question of what the sufficient (as distinguished from necessary) condition for psychopathology may be, since in this case brain change is only necessary, not sufficient. Nonetheless, this model implies a "harder" brain substrate than the above model whereby altered brain organization temporally follows psychopathology. The further implication is that certain types or loci of brain disorders must be particularly critical for psychopathological symptomatology (Haracz 1982). This, in turn, invites a mapping of psychiatric symptoms and syndromes on to particular regions of brain abnormality, in much the same way that classical aphasiologists sought to map disordered language (and, later, normal language processes) onto brain topography.

In either case, given the wide individual differences in human physiology as well as behavior, there is no particular reason to assume that the variance in brain states, within a given syndrome of psychopathology, should be less than the variance of behavioral manifestations in that form of psychopathology. There is also no particular reason to assume that the variance in brain states in a particular form of psychopathology, under conditions of a particular task activation or state induction, should be less than the variance that would be induced in normals by the same task or state. In a review, Seidman (1983) has noted that many neurological and metabolic disorders have been associated with schizophrenic-like symptoms. In the case where brain change precedes behavioral change, the assumption would be that either of several dysfunctions in the system could produce a similar behavioral result, particularly if the several sites of dysfunction are part of some serial processing system. (In aphasia, for example, certain thalamic lesions produce syndromes that are similar to some of the classical cortical syndromes.) In the contrary case, where psychopathology precedes brain change, there is the concept of a system that is literally breaking apart, with no plausible reason why the topography of brokenness should be identical or even similar in similarly diagnosed individuals. A row of Humpty Dumptys falling off a wall would not be expected to show the same fracture patterns.

It is thus an empirical question whether individual differences in brain activity in a psychopathological group would be greater or less than the differences among normals in a comparable state or task. The particular form of the data, however, might raise a variety of etiological and natural history possibilities, as described above.

PRELIMINARY FINDINGS

Method

We present here results from the use of a recognition memory activation paradigm, with regional cerebral blood flow measurements made by the xenon-133 inhalation method. Forty-four concrete nouns were presented through earphones to the subjects, each word repeated once and all words spaced 2.5 seconds apart. Subjects were asked to repeat the word each time it was said, within the interstimulus interval. A list of 88 words was then presented through the phones, with the previous 44 words randomly embedded. Subjects used a bimanual finger-lift response to indicate if the word being heard was from the previous list. The first regional cerebral blood flow measurement was made during this recognition trial. Two subsequent training and recognition trials were presented, using the same list, in a manner identical to the first training and recognition trial. The third of the recognition trials was also accompanied by blood flow measurements. This allowed a comparison of earlier and later stages in the learning of the list.

A group of 40 normal adults, ages 21 through 44 years, 20 men and 20 women, served as the control population for this report. The men and women did not differ significantly in age, years of education, and accuracy of task performance. We report also on 8 female bipolars tested in the manic phase, 5 female bipolars tested in the depressed phase, and 11 male schizophrenics. All had at least a 10-day withdrawal from neuroleptic medication and met research diagnostic criteria (SADS-RDC) for their diagnosis at time of testing.

Memory Deficit Common to Mania, Depression, and Schizophrenia

The first finding was simply that the recognition memory task revealed deficient performance in all three psychopathological groups.

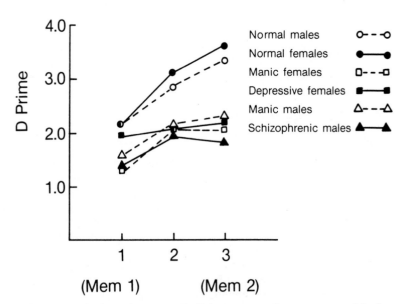

Figure 1. Task performance (D Prime) across three memory trials for normal subjects and groups with psychiatric diagnoses.

Indeed, not only was the performance deficient, but it was roughly equally so for all three groups. Gur and colleagues have reported similar performance deficits for medicated and unmedicated schizophrenics (1983, 1985) and for medicated depressives (1984) on a verbal analogies test. There may be subtle differences in the slope of the learning curve among the three groups, but these are clearly less dramatic than the major difference between normal controls on the one hand and all psychopathological groups on the other hand (Figure 1).

This first result is itself interesting, since deficient mnestic or attentional performance, as measured by this task, has often been described as inherent in one or the other of these types of psychopathology, but seldom has such deficient performance been attributed in this nonspecific way to all three groups.

The result also sets the stage for an analysis along the lines described above, in which the variances of brain activity between and within

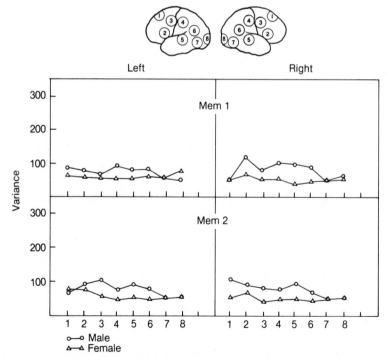

Figure 2. Normal male and female variance by site and hemisphere.

diagnostic groups become a major question. Is this similar behavioral state of deficient memory accompanied by a brain state that is similar across diagnostic groups, or are there group-specific brain activity patterns that accompany this behavior? Even more basically, is there important (greater than normal) within-group variance in any of the psychopathological groups?

Within-Group Variances

In those patients with depression and mania, there were striking increases in variance as compared to normal controls, even in these relatively small groups (Figures 2–5). Given the small groups, it is hazardous to conclude too much from the site-by-site landscape or profile of variances. The exception to this may be the diminution of variance for depressives on the second memory trial, particularly in the right-temporal and parietal areas. The logic of the analysis would say that this suggests a commonality among depressives that emerges

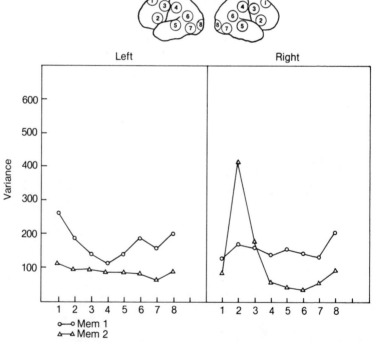

Figure 3. Comparison of variance for bipolar depressive women across memory trials.

only with repetition of the learning task, and most especially in the right hemisphere. It is interesting, then, to notice that depressives may have an even flatter learning curve than the other groups—as though repeated learning trials more consistently evoked their deficit (Figure 1). While that may indeed speak to extant theories about the locus of brain dysfunction in depression, it leaves open the question of why depressives should be so variable at the initial stages of learning.

The findings for the manic group were even more consistently abnormal, across sites and across memory trials, than the findings for the depressive group. While there is again a suggestion of intersite variance differences, the more prominent fact is the significantly higher variance in the manic group across all sites. No single region uniformly characterized manic patients during recognition memory performance. Again, inspection reveals wide variance not only in

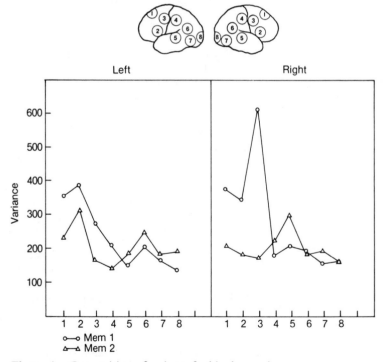

Figure 4. Comparision of variance for bipolar manic women across memory trials.

absolute flow values, but also in profiles or patterns of flow across sites.

The implication of such high within-group variance is unmistakable: no single brain state is characteristic of mania, even when subjects are engaged in a task at which they are relatively uniformly impaired. A consistent behavioral state of memory impairment is apparently not the result of a single, consistent neural process.

Is there anything at all that can be considered inherent to the manic syndrome? Yes, but it would seem from these data to be a process that gives rise to multiple manifestations of disinhibited neural or behavioral control. Loss of control itself may be fundamental to the syndrome. That forces the burden of explanation and subsequent research in an interesting new direction. The question then becomes: Can disinhibition be a sufficient cause for manic behavior, or is some

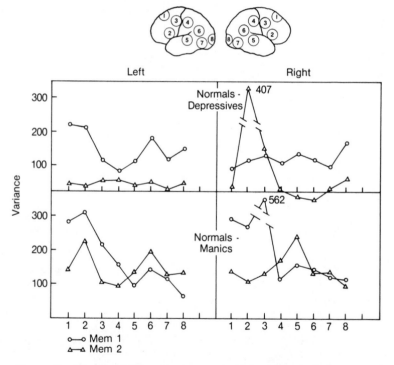

Figure 5. Variance differences across memory tasks comparing normal women to bipolar depressive and bipolar manic women (positive values indicate greater variance in psychiatric groups).

biasing force required to explain the predominant euphoria? Is happiness simply a loose brain?

The findings for schizophrenic subjects, on the other hand, offer a contrasting picture (Figure 6). Here there was a level of variance no higher than normal and—as in normal controls—relatively uniform across sites. Since the variance patterns revealed no abnormality, the means became interpretable. If they differed from normal, some conclusions could legitimately be drawn about levels and pattern of flow that generally characterize schizophrenia. That brings us to the final considerations from the data, namely, the means themselves.

Differences in Means Among
Psychopathological and Normal Groups

Given the variance differences, it is especially significant that the affectively disordered groups have means that are lower, rather than higher, than normal (Figures 7–11). Mathew et al. (1980) have also

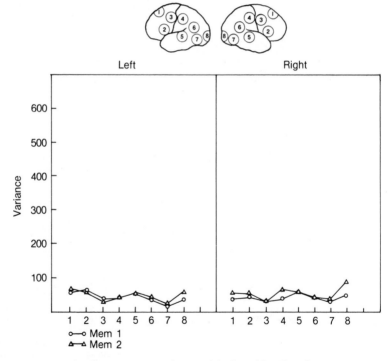

Figure 6. Variances across memory trials for schizophrenic men.

reported bilateral decreases in the blood flow of depressives. Given the high variability in the affective group, it will be fascinating if this relationship holds up in a larger sample since, as discussed in the first section of this report, such a result is distinctly uncommon in the literature; the usual case is that higher variances are accompanied by higher, not lower, means. This can only be interpreted as reflecting the operation of two different forces: one that induces disinhibited variability among the patients and another that pushes this variable group toward lower flows. It is especially interesting that mania was in many cases accompanied by flows that were even lower than those

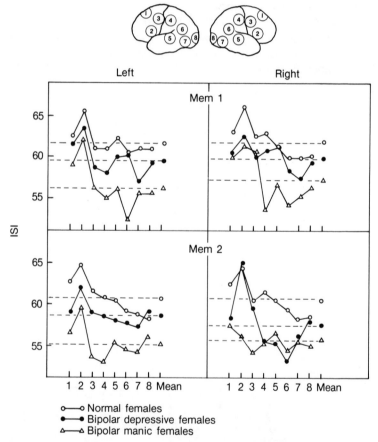

Figure 7. Mean flow for normal, bipolar depressive, and bipolar manic women.

in depression (in agreement with Gustafson et al. 1981). This suggests that loss of control may typically mean loss of activation. In turn, that would imply that euphoria is a sort of default state of the organism—the condition it assumes when it is relatively unconstrained and underactivated.

On the second memory trial the depressive group was, as noted above, no more than normally variable in the right-hemisphere temporal and parietal areas. It is then noteworthy that the means for those regions also showed the most reduction from normal, leading to the possibility that a focal deficit in this region may indeed be involved. That conforms to recent suggestions by Tucker (Chapter

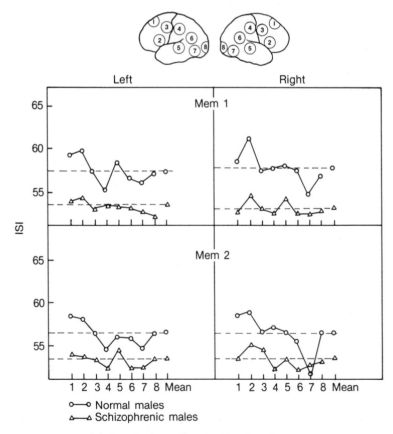

Figure 8. Mean flow for normal and schizophrenic men.

6) and others. It certainly leaves open the important question of why that deficit only appears in the later stage of memory.

By contrast, as has also been observed by Mathew et al. (1982), the schizophrenic group showed a generally lower mean flow, particularly in the left-temporal areas, where there was a flattening of the normal peak of activation during the initial memory trial. The significance of this finding is enhanced by the fact that—on the first trial—this left-temporal site was the only one correlated with task accuracy and vocabulary in normal controls. Thus there may be a valid focal deficit, generally characteristic of schizophrenia and relevant to the memory task deficit. For purposes of the present discussion, the findings for schizophrenia are important in establishing that the variability findings in affective disorder are not necessarily inherent in all forms of psychopathology.

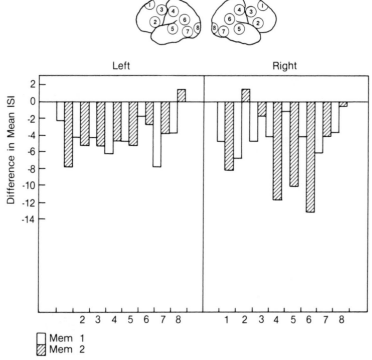

Figure 9. Mean differences comparing normal women and bipolar depressive women (negative values indicate lower means in depressive subjects).

CONCLUSION

As an initial report of work in progress, we offer the above information to illustrate the method and the typical findings. Obviously, they need replication and extension, but already they seem to provide some interesting new directions for hypotheses to be tested. We summarize our findings as follows.

1. Probe recognition memory, after repeated trials, is a nonspecific area of deficit, common to both phases of bipolar affective disorder and to schizophrenia. This should force a consideration of two possibilities, one practical and one theoretical. Practically, it should stimulate the use of memory tests as sensitive neuropsychological

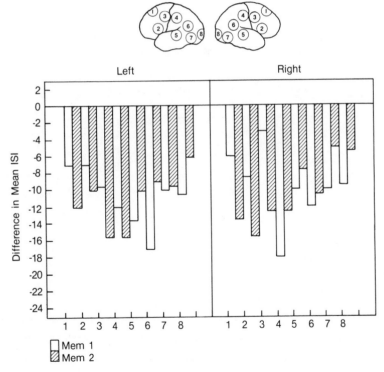

Figure 10. Mean differences comparing normal women and bipolar manic women (negative values indicate lower means in manic subjects).

assessment instruments. It has often been observed that memory tests are sensitive to brain injury, and memory is usually the first process to be affected in cases of progressing brain disease. In the same way, it may be such tests that will be useful in the sensitive detection of psychopathology.

From a theoretical point of view, the next natural question is about the various pathways to this common memory deficit. It is an uncommon and interesting theoretical situation: Whereas one usually thinks of diverse psychopathologies as originating from, and deviating from, a common prior state of normality, this is a case where diverse psychopathologies converge on a common outcome of shared deficit. That common outcome provides a fortuitous control or anchor for studying the various pathological mechanisms of the deficit—a control that is not avail-

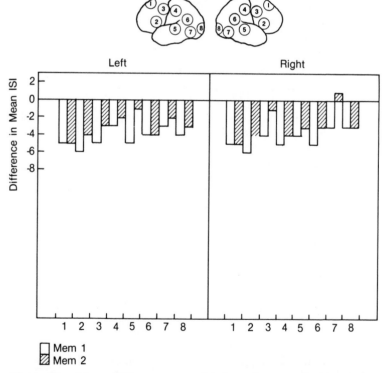

Figure 11. Mean differences comparing normal men and schizophrenic men (negative values indicate lower means for schizophrenics).

able either within the diverse phenomenology of the psycho-pathological syndromes or within the prior premorbid attributes of the patients.

2. Variability of cortical activation levels and patterns, even within the relatively constrained circumstances of the memory paradigm, apparently a hallmark of the manic state, may be a prominent feature of depression in the initial stages of learning. For the central purposes of this volume, namely, a clarification of the cerebral basis of depressed affect, these observations suggest that depression will best "settle in" to a characteristic neuropsychological state only after repeated learning trials. In the early stages, the subjects might then be less constrained by their depression (or, to put it another way, novelty may to some extent counteract the chronically deleterious effects of depression on memory). In the initial stages, then, as Figure 1 suggests, depression is accompanied by less abnormality than mania.

3. In the later stages of repetitive learning, a more stable pattern of generally lower flows is found in depression. The lower flows do appear to be especially prominent in the right-temporal and parietal areas, and this may suggest that such regions do become disproportionately dysfunctional at that stage of the learning process. On the other hand, the dysfunction there has state properties related to the task history; it might, therefore, not be a uniform characteristic of depression.

4. Finally, simply in terms of blood flow levels, it appears that the depressed phase of bipolar disease does not represent as severe a deficit in brain activation as is represented by the manic phase. The relatively less normal mean flow values seen in the manic phase may help explain why unipolar depression is possible, but not unipolar mania: in this model, one could cycle back and forth between depression and normality without encountering mania.

A psychological implication may also be derived from this observation of the relatively more normal brain activation of depression. There may be more "work" going on in the depressed state than in the manic state. Some of the symptomatology of depression, particularly the negative self-attributions, might then be the result of such work—hence a greater likelihood in depression than in mania that cognitive therapy can successfully redirect this work.

REFERENCES

Gur RE, Skolnick BE, Gur RC, et al: Brain function in psychiatric disorders, I: regional cerebral blood flow in medicated schizophrenics. Arch Gen Psychiatry 40:1250–1254, 1983

Gur RE, Skolnick BE, Gur RC, et al: Brain function in psychiatric disorders, II: regional cerebral blood flow in medicated unipolar depressives. Arch Gen Psychiatry 41:695–699, 1984

Gur RE, Gur RC, Skolnick BE, et al: Brain function in psychiatric disorders, III: regional cerebral blood flow in unmedicated schizophrenics. Arch Gen Psychiatry 42:329–334, 1985

Gustafson L, Risberg J, Silfverskiold P: Regional cerebral blood flow in organic dementia and affective disorders. Adv Biol Psychiatry 6:109–116, 1981

Haracz JL: The dopamine hypothesis; An overview of studies with schizophrenic patients. Schizophr Bull 8:438–469, 1982

Jensen TS, Genefke IK, Hyldebrandt N, et al: Cerebral atrophy in young torture victims. N Engl J Med 307:1341, 1983

Kellner CH, Roy-Byrne PP, Rubinow DR, et al: Cerebral atrophy in young torture victims. N Engl J Med 308:903, 1983

Mathew RJ, Meyer JS, Francis DJ: Cerebral blood flow in depression. Am J Psychiatry 137:1449–1450, 1980

Mathew RJ, Duncan GC, Weinman ML: Regional cerebral blood flow in schizophrenia. Arch Gen Psychiatry 39:1121–1124, 1982

Seidman L: Schizophrenia and brain dysfunction: an integration of recent neurodiagnostic findings. Psychol Bull 94:195–238, 1983

Wood F: Laterality of cerebral function: its investigation by measurement of localized brain activity, in Cerebral Functional Asymmetry: Method and Theory. Edited by Hellige J. New York, Praeger, 1982

Chapter 6

Neuropsychological Mechanisms of Affective Self-Regulation

Don M. Tucker, Ph.D.

Chapter 6

Neuropsychological Mechanisms of Affective Self-Regulation

Conventional approaches to depression have described either biological or psychological causes. There have been few attempts to reason from the neural level to the psychological level. This fragmentation of theoretical understanding has led to a fragmentation of clinical practice. Some clinicians treat depression as a disorder of brain chemistry, others as a result of maladaptive thinking. Because both kinds of treatment may be effective, and because there is little evidence by which to distinguish a biological or endogenous depression from a psychological one, it seems likely that the real advances in our understanding will come only when we consider these approaches not as competing alternative theories, but as parallel descriptions, both of which are incomplete.

The task for a neuropsychological theory of depression is to describe brain and mind in the same terms. Although this task is certainly formidable, there is an air of excitement now among many researchers—a sense that we are close to an understanding of brain function that may shed new light on the nature of human emotion and psychopathology. The neuropsychological approach brings ideas and evidence from one level of analysis to the other. At the psychological level we have an increasing body of evidence on the nature of cognitive-affective interactions in depression. This evidence poses specific questions about emotional arousal, attention, and cognitive evaluation that theories of neural systems must address if they are to be relevant. At the neural level, we have increasing evidence on how specific brain systems contribute to such psychological phenomena as inappropriate cheerfulness or orientation to hedonic stimuli. This evidence shows that some traditional psychological theories of emotion are untenable, and it sets the stage for interesting new ways of thinking. With an increasing number of constraints at the psychological and neural levels, there are correspondingly fewer theoretical models that work at both levels.

In this chapter I will begin by reviewing evidence on differential left- and right-hemisphere function in emotion. Although there are major interpretive problems raised by this evidence, it provides a framework through which neuropsychological changes in depression might be understood not as a disease process, but as exaggerations of normal affective self-regulatory mechanisms.

The lateral dimension of brain organization has been the central one in recent thinking on brain and emotion, but it has become necessary to consider the front-back and up-down dimensions of brain organization as well. Interpreting a hemisphere's contribution to an emotional state has become difficult without having some notion of how frontal lobe activity relates to posterior hemispheric cognitive processes. And the left-right and front-back dimensions both apply to cortical representations of affect: it is also necessary to consider limbic and brainstem control systems that play major roles in the affective modulation of cortical function.

In considering each of these perspectives on neural systems, I will relate the neuropsychological theorizing to conventional psychological theories of emotion, in an attempt to share constraints across levels. The approach will be to frame theoretical issues broadly rather than review evidence in detail. The main question is where to look for depressive affect in the brain. Is it to be found in the cognitive operations of the cortex? If so, is it on the right? In the front? Or is depressive affect more properly traced to the more primitive regulation of memory by adaptive mechanisms of the limbic system? Or even to the elementary arousal controls in the brainstem? The psychological findings and theories can provide clues to guide this search. In turn, where we find the cerebral representation of depressive affect may show whether depression arises out of complex mechanisms of cognitive appraisal or whether it reflects some more primitive mechanisms of neural self-regulation.

DEPRESSION AND HEMISPHERIC
SPECIALIZATION FOR EMOTION

One of the most important findings on emotion and brain function in the last few years has been that the right hemisphere of most right-handers is specialized for the cognitive processing of emotional communications. The most consistent evidence has been gathered for comprehension of nonverbal emotional messages. Patients with right-hemisphere lesions may show impaired understanding of emotion conveyed in facial expressions (Borod et al. 1986) or in tone of voice (Tucker et al. 1976). Research with normals using unilateral stimulus presentation has confirmed right-hemisphere specialization for understanding nonverbal emotional messages (Safer and Leventhal 1977; Ley and Bryden 1979).

The findings on expression of emotions have been somewhat more complex, but are generally consistent with those for comprehension abilities. Observations of patients with certain right-hemisphere lesions (Ross and Mesulam 1979) have suggested that they may be impaired in the ability to modulate speech with appropriate affective intonation. Normal persons have been found to express emotions more intensely on the left side of the face (Campbell 1978; Sackeim et al. 1978), suggesting right-hemisphere facilitation of the facial display of emotion. Although some researchers have suggested that the left-sided intensity of facial expression might be stronger for negative emotions (Sackeim et al. 1978), and others argued that the left-sided effect is found only for posed facial expressions (Ekman et al. 1981), the research now seems to suggest that the left-sided intensity is observed for positive as well as negative emotions and spontaneous as well as posed expressions (Borod et al. 1986; Dopson et al. 1984).

The findings of a more intense expression of emotion on the left side of the face has been assumed to reflect the right hemisphere's facilitation of emotional expression. Yet traditional neurological observations have shown that cortical lesions impair voluntary facial movements, but may disinhibit spontaneous emotional displays contralaterally (Monrad-Krohn 1924). Thus an alternative explanation is that the facial asymmetry is produced by greater inhibitory control by the left hemisphere on the right side of the face (Dopson et al. 1984). This explanation is consistent with other evidence of a left-hemisphere role in emotional inhibition (Buck and Duffy 1980; Buck 1985; Tucker and Newman 1981). A better understanding of cortical inhibitory influences may be necessary to explain the maturation of lateral brain function and emotion in infants, in whom facial expressions of emotion are more intense on the right side of the face (Best 1986; Rothbart et al., manuscript in preparation).

Although much of the literature on lateralization and emotion is focused on which hemisphere does what, thus dealing primarily with the question of localization of function, the real significance of this work may be that it clarifies the substantial cognitive processing required to communicate emotion effectively. And although the verbal, propositional cognitive skills of the left hemisphere are certainly important to this task, what we have learned most from this research is that nonverbal emotional communication is not automatic, but requires the perceptual and conceptual skills of the right hemisphere. In contrast to the left hemisphere's linguistic functions based on information processing with a substitutive semantic code—words—the right hemisphere's cognition is analogical—the internal representation is an analog of perceptual experience.

Here we may find a clue on the cerebral representation of depressive affect: the representational form for many examples of affective behavior seems to be analogical. When a clinician interprets a patient's tone of voice as depressed, that manifestation of depression is represented in analog form both in the clinician's brain and in the patient's. Furthermore, we can localize this manifestation of depressive affect to the right hemisphere.

Can we then conclude that depressed affect itself is represented in the right hemisphere? There is another kind of evidence on brain lateralization and emotion, and it has most often been interpreted to provide an affirmative answer to this question. This evidence has a long and controversial history. One early event in this history was Goldstein's (1952) observation that depressive-catastrophic emotional responses were more frequent with left- than right-hemisphere lesions. While a negative response to experiencing brain damage is not surprising, it was also observed that right-hemisphere damage may alter emotional functioning, but in an opposite fashion, producing a tendency to deny the seriousness of the impairment. Gainotti's (1972) systematic observations of emotional effects of unilateral brain lesions confirmed a general tendency for patients to show a greater incidence of denial after right-hemisphere damage.

The unilateral lesion data present a different picture of emotion in the brain from the studies of nonverbal communication. They seem to suggest that there is hemispheric specialization for positive versus negative emotions. If we assume that after a unilateral lesion, the patient's emotional response reflects the influence of the intact hemisphere, then these findings would indicate that the left hemisphere has a more positive emotional orientation, and the right is more negative (see Sackheim et al. 1982). This is the most straightforward interpretation of these findings, and this interpretation has been influential on many recent studies of lateralization and emotion.

However, it is not necessarily the case that a brain lesion decreases the functioning of a neural system. We have seen above that a cortical lesion may disinhibit that hemisphere's control of the facial expression of emotion (Monrad-Krohn 1924). Hall et al. (1968) proposed an ipsilateral disinhibition interpretation to explain the effects of a hemispheric lesion on the patient's responses to the Rorschach inkblot test. In reviewing the literature on lateralization and emotion, I found this interpretation of the lesion evidence to be most consistent with the hemisphere's emotional orientations when all the available evidence was considered (Tucker 1981). This interpretation would suggest that the depressive-catastrophic response reflects an exaggeration of the left hemisphere's normal emotional orientation, whereas the denial of problems shown with right-hemisphere lesions may reflect a pathological exaggeration of the right hemisphere's normal contribution to emotional functioning.

The research on hemispheric specialization for emotion thus presents two major lines of evidence. One suggests that the right hemisphere's nonverbal cognitive skills are important to emotional communication. The other suggests that there may be a lateralized representation of positive versus negative emotion, but which hemisphere is associated with positive and which with negative emotions is controversial. In attempting to understand the hemispheres' emotional characteristics, which are relatively unknown, it may be important to rely on what is known about their cognitive characteristics. Traditional psychological theories of emotion have proposed that human emotion takes form only through a process of cognitive appraisal or attribution. Considering the two hemispheres' differing cognitive characteristics may provide new ways of thinking about this process.

THE TOP-DOWN VIEW IN PSYCHOLOGICAL THEORIES OF EMOTION AND DEPRESSION

The primary approach of psychological theories of emotion has been to emphasize what might be called the top-down view, in which emotions are seen to arise as the outcome of cognitive appraisals of life events (for a review of current concepts of emotion, see Leventhal and Tomarken 1986). This top-down approach was first articulated in modern psychology in James's (1884) interpretation that our experience of bodily feelings has emotional significance only when we interpret these feelings with respect to the environmental context. Although Cannon (1929) believed he had discounted visceral theories of emotion when he showed that emotional reactions remained after the visceral nerves were severed, psychologists have continued to understand physiological arousal in terms of visceral, rather than central, mechanisms. Schacter and Singer (1962) gave subjects epinephrine injections and showed that the resulting emotional reactions depended on the psychological context in which the increased autonomic arousal was interpreted. Even today, Mandler's (1985) model proposes that there is no specificity to emotional experience except that which arises from a mixture of cognitive attributions and diffuse autonomic nervous system activity.

Lazarus (1982) also emphasizes that emotions are created through the cognitive appraisal of the meaning of life events. Zajonc (1982), however, has taken issue with the cognitive primacy model. He argues that certain emotional responses—such as the judgment as to whether we like an object—occur before any cognitive processes. Although Zajonc's challenge has raised the question of just how elaborate a cognitive appraisal must be before an emotional response develops, the dominant view of emotion in current psychological theory is still that our cognitive appraisals of events determine what our feelings will be.

It must be kept in mind that the acceptance of cognitive processes as valid topics for scientific inquiry has only occurred in the last few decades in American psychology. It is perhaps not surprising, then, that psychologists would use cognitive explanations as they attempted to understand emotions.

This emphasis on cognition has been the mode in psychological theories of depression as well. Although there have been attempts to integrate multiple factors in the etiology of depression, including negative affective response to life events and changes in attention with depressed affect (Lewinsohn, in press), the dominant view has been that maladaptive cognition causes depression. This view forms the basis of the cognitive therapy for depression proposed by Beck et al. (1979). The depressed person is seen to distort experiences in a way that increases the likelihood of a depressed affective response. This view is also expressed in the reformulated learned-helplessness model of depression (Abramson et al. 1978), which holds that the characteristics of the cognitive attributions a person makes about outcomes of life events—such as whether a negative outcome is attributed to a personal, internal cause rather than to an external one—determine the incidence of depression.

If we accept this top-down view, in which cognition causes depressive affect, a neuropsychological theory may offer interesting ways of specifying the nature of the cognitive operations through which depressive affect is generated and handled. What is the nature of the cognitive representation of causal attributions? In most examples, the form of the representation seems to be verbal: the subject "labels" the autonomic arousal as humor or anger. Cognitive therapy for depression often focuses specifically on self-statements: private verbalizations. It is difficult to conceive of attributions about the cause of the outcomes of life events in other than verbal terms.

Certainly both private and public verbalizations are important in the appraisal processes that determine the shape an emotional response will take. But there seems to have been an assumption in psychology that higher mental processes are verbally mediated, perhaps not unlike the assumption in traditional neurology that the higher mental processes are carried out by the left hemisphere. The recognition of the importance of the right hemisphere in nonverbal emotional communication raises the possibility that its analogical cognitive skills may be important in the experience of emotion as well.

Safer and Leventhal (1977) emphasized that in the experience of emotion a variety of introceptive and perceptual cues must be integrated. They proposed that the right hemisphere's holistic abilities may be particularly suited to this integration. Drawing from Heinz Werner's cognitive developmental theory, I suggested that the right hemisphere may be important to syncretic experience, in which emotions, body posture, and sensory data are fused in an undifferentiated percept (Tucker 1981). More recently, Buck (1985) has developed this notion further, proposing that an important function of emotional systems in the brain is to provide a direct readout of current affective status to the cognitive systems; the syncretic conceptualization of the right hemisphere may be the vehicle through which this readout is accomplished. Lazarus (1986) has recently considered the possibility that syncretic cognition may provide a fast and direct form of cognitive appraisal that helps to determine emotional experience. I have proposed that because the internal representation of the perception of nonverbal emotional communications is in a syncretic, analogical form, there may be an experiential immediacy of nonverbal communication—whereby it accesses the perceiver's own affective semantics directly—that may not occur for verbal communication (Tucker 1986).

As we recognize the importance of analogical cognitive representation in emotion, does this suggest new ways of thinking about depression? Does the depressed person's right hemisphere perform some distorted apprehension of nonverbal interpersonal cues that parallels the maladaptive verbal representation of causal attributions? Can we interpret the unilateral lesion evidence to suggest that there is a generally negative emotional tone to the right hemisphere, such that the depressed person experiences an exaggerated negative affective response to life?

I think we may learn much about the experience of depressed affect by studying the right hemisphere's syncretic conceptual process. But interpreting the existing evidence on the right hemisphere's role in depression is complicated. There have been some suggestions of increased right-hemisphere functioning in depression. However, a consistent finding has been that right-hemisphere cognitive and perceptual abilities are impaired during a state of depressive affect. Furthermore, there are some indications that an increased contribution of the right hemisphere in a person's cognitive style is associated with a positive cognitive bias.

DEPRESSION AND HEMISPHERIC COGNITION

So far, we have considered how the two hemispheres' differing cognitive characteristics may provide differing ways of cognitively handling emotional responses. It may also prove helpful to consider the hemispheres' cognitive characteristics as we interpret evidence relevant to lateralization of positive and negative emotion. Whether or not a hemisphere's cognitive functioning is increased or decreased can provide an indication of whether that hemisphere is more or less activated in a given affective state.

Some of the earliest evidence that asymmetries in brain function are important to depression came from electroencephalogram (EEG) studies. Perris (1975) observed that EEG abnormalities in depressed patients were more pronounced over the right hemisphere. Data from event-related potentials confirmed these early indications (Perris 1974). More recently, Von Knorring (1984) has shown that right-hemisphere EEG changes may be related to the depressed patient's neuroendocrine response on the dexamethasone suppression test, a response that may index the severity of depression.

Another influential early finding was Flor-Henry's (1969) observation that affective disorders were more frequent in patients with right-temporal-lobe epilepsy than in those with left-temporal-lobe epilepsy. As with the EEG findings, the implication seemed to be that there is some dysfunction of the right hemisphere that is related to depression. Flor-Henry and associates investigated this implication by conducting a neuropsychological assessment of depressed psychiatric patients; results showed poor visuospatial performance suggestive of right-hemisphere dysfunction (for a review see Flor-Henry 1979).

Some findings of right-lateralized abnormalities in depressed patients would seem to suggest exaggerated, rather than decreased, activation of the right hemisphere in depression—a result that would be consistent with the contralateral release interpretation of the unilateral lesion evidence. Depressed patients were found by Schweitzer (1979) and Myslobodsky and Horesh (1978) to show a high proportion of left lateral eye movements while thinking, a possible indication of increased right-hemisphere activation. Electrodermal recordings have shown depressed subjects to have asymmetrical responses between the hands (Gruzelier and Venables 1974). Although the neural mediation of electrodermal responses is not known, Gruzelier

(1986) has reasoned from several lines of evidence to suggest that these data reflect overaction of the right hemisphere in depression.

While interpreting relative hemispheric activation from some measures of asymmetry in depression has been difficult, a consistent finding has been that right-hemisphere cognitive and perceptual function is impaired in depressed patients—at least while they are depressed. Some investigators who were not aware of a laterality hypothesis have reported poor right-hemisphere performance on neuropsychological tests (Goldstein et al. 1977; Kronfol et al. 1978). This pattern of neuropsychological-test findings would seem to suggest that depression involves some kind of right-hemisphere brain damage. Yet remember that when the depressive-catastrophic response occurs after known brain lesions, it follows left- rather than right-hemisphere damage. Furthermore, in some cases follow-up testing showed that for patients in whom treatment produced an improvement in mood, right-hemisphere performance returned to normal. A particularly striking finding was the presence of poor visuospatial performance and left-sided soft signs in depressed children, both of which normalized after tricyclic therapy (Brumback et al. 1980).

The possibility that there may be a dynamic covariance of right-hemisphere function with mood level has also been suggested by experimental induction of a depressed mood in normal subjects. My associates and I induced a depressed mood in college students and found an impairment of visual imagery and an auditory attentional bias favoring the right ear; we interpreted these as indicating decreased performance of the right hemisphere during the depressed mood (Tucker et al. 1981). Our EEG recordings did not show the kind of abnormalities found by Perris et al. (1978) for depressed patients, but rather showed an unexpected increase in cortical activation, indicated by alpha suppression, over the right-frontal lobe. In an attempt to explain the apparent discrepancy between right-hemisphere cognitive and attentional impairment and increased frontal EEG activation, we speculated that perhaps depressive affect involves an inhibition from frontal structures that suppresses more posterior regions of the right hemisphere. In more recent work (Tucker and Dawson 1984), we did not replicate the frontal-lobe asymmetry, but did find right-hemisphere EEG changes as a function of mood. We asked method actors to create emotions of depression or sexual arousal in the laboratory. When they reported sexual arousal we found greater right- than left-hemisphere activation indicated by EEG alpha desynchronization; during depression they showed less right- than left-hemisphere activation.

Recently, Liotti et al. (manuscript in preparation) have observed impairment of right-hemisphere attentional performance in depressed psychiatric patients. The patients showed particularly slow reaction times to stimuli presented to the left visual half-field. Repeating this experiment with normal subjects who were asked to maintain a depressed mood during the experiment, Ladavas et al. (1984) found a similar left-visual-field, right-hemisphere performance decrement.

These findings with normal subjects raise some difficult but intriguing questions. Some of these questions—such as the role of frontal-lobe activity and the transient nature of right-hemisphere changes in depressive affect—will be taken up later in this chapter. With respect to the goal of using hemispheric cognitive function as a marker to index greater or lesser hemispheric function in depressive affect, the majority of the findings with both depressed and normal persons suggest that—at least for the cognitive representational functions of the posterior right hemisphere—depression is associated with decreased right-hemisphere function.

Another line of evidence may suggest that an increase of right-hemisphere contribution to the person's cognitive functioning is associated with a more positive affect. In traditional clinical psychological formulations of personality disorders, there are descriptions of global versus analytic cognitive styles (Shapiro 1965) that seem to resemble hemispheric cognitive processes. In the obsessive-compulsive personality, whose rigid intellectualization and penchant for detail suggest a left-hemisphere cognitive style, we find a restricted affective life with something of a negative tone. Is this a characterization of an exaggerated left hemisphere in personality? In the hysteric personality, on the other hand, whose global and undifferentiated cognitive style suggests relatively greater right-hemisphere contribution, we find affective lability, a tendency to deny problems, and Pollyannish optimism. Are these the affective characteristics that emerge when the right hemisphere makes the major contribution to personality organization?

It is not clear whether there are real differences in brain function between these personality types, although there is an interesting finding that conversion disorders are more frequent on the left side of the body (Galin et al. 1977; Kenyon 1964). The association of an increased right-hemisphere psychological influence with optimism and denial of problems has been observed in a condition where laterality is known: right-temporal-lobe epilepsy. Bear and Fedio (1977) found that temporal-lobe epileptics with a focus on the right scored higher on an "affective" psychometric factor, whereas those with a left focus scored higher on an "ideative" factor. These findings were consistent with the notion that temporal-lobe epilepsy exaggerates some aspects of a hemisphere's functioning in the person's personality. When comparing the patient's self-descriptions with reports from observers, Bear and Fedio found that the left-focus patients exaggerated their negative qualities, while the right-focus patients denied problems and portrayed themselves in a more favorable light than did the observers.

Do these findings suggest different roles for the hemispheres in self-evaluation? When we find a negative self-evaluation bias in a depressed person, is this another reflection of a decreased contribution from the right hemisphere in the person's mental functioning? Some preliminary evidence that this might be the case was provided by Swensen and Tucker (1983). We related scores on Zenhausern's test of hemispheric cognitive style to a self-report scale of emotion: subjects reporting a more right- than left-hemisphere cognitive style reported less timidity (anxiety), less depression, and showed more positive self-report bias on a social desirability scale.

Other observations of normal students by Levy et al. (1983) show interesting parallels to these trends when subjects evaluated their performance on a visual half-field task. Levy et al. found that some subjects showed a strong right-field bias on a syllable identification task; others showed a weak effect or no effect. Levy et al. interpreted these hemisphere performance patterns to indicate characteristic individual differences in hemispheric activation. Those with the strong right-field bias might be thought of as left-hemisphere types. When asked to rate their performance, all subjects were fairly accurate in rating right-field (left-hemisphere) performance, and they were less accurate in rating left-field (right-hemisphere) performance. In rating left-field performance, those subjects characterized by greater left-hemisphere activation showed a bias to be self-critical, while those with greater right-hemisphere activation rated themselves as having done better than they had. In discussing these and other findings, Levy (1982) suggests they are consistent with the interpretation that persons with characteristic left-hemisphere activation are more introverted, while those tending toward right-hemisphere activation are more extroverted; along with greater affective lability and expressivity, the extrovert shows an optimistic emotional orientation.

INTRAHEMISPHERIC RELATIONS

So far in this chapter, as in much of the neuropsychological research on emotion, the unit of analysis has been the hemisphere. While a hemisphere has proven to be an interesting level of explanation in many ways, a more precise analysis may be necessary to resolve some of the discrepant interpretations. It may not be long before we recognize that each major region of the cortex plays a role in emotional functioning (see Kolb and Taylor 1986). But for now it is necessary at least to differentiate between anterior and posterior systems within a hemisphere. This yields a quadrant model of the cortical representation of emotion, with emotional stability achieved not only through a balance between differing right- and left-hemisphere orientations, but through each hemisphere's modulation of its functioning through a balance between anterior and posterior regions.

It is important to consider the functional differentiation between anterior and posterior cortex. Although ignored by emotion theorists except Pribram (1981), and now Kinsbourne and Bemporad (in press), this differentiation provides some important ways of understanding emotional processes. Posterior cortex contains the primary sensory projection fields, and the higher-order integration of these. It specializes in what we might call *representative* functions—represention of information about the environmental context. Pribram (1981) describes this as the brain's *participatory* mode, in which it participates in the qualities of the environmental context.

For anterior-cortical regions, there are two kinds of function to consider. The first is motor organization. This is important because there may be inherent affective qualities to the neural control systems that modulate motor readiness. The second kind of anterior brain function is what might be called a *regulatory* function. There are substantial back-and-forth connections between each major cortical region and frontal cortex (Nauta 1971). Recent positron emission tomographic studies suggest that each of the cognitive operations of posterior cortex is paralleled by activity in a specific prefrontal (non-motor) site (Roland 1984). Because of the substantial interconnections between prefrontal cortex and limbic structures, it has been thought for some time that frontal cortex is involved in some kind of executive operations in service of adaptive needs. Pribram (1981) provides an important developmental perspective: throughout the evolution of the nervous system, certain structures have specialized to handle representation of external data, while others have handled homeostatic functions like pain response and temperature regulation. These regulatory functions seem to receive their highest elaboration in the human brain in the frontal cortex.

As we attempt to characterize hemispheric cognitive function in emotion, it may be that we are describing more posterior, representative functions. There are several indications that there may be a reciprocity between anterior and posterior cortical systems within a hemisphere, such that increased posterior representative functioning is associated with a decrease in the regulatory control from frontal cortex.

In the study of a depressed mood in normal subjects, my associates and I observed increased frontal-lobe activation in the EEG record when behavioral data suggested a decrement in right-hemisphere performance (Tucker et al. 1981). Independently, Davidson (1978, 1984; also Chapter 1 in this volume) had observed a similar phenomenon. While viewing a videotape, subjects reported their emotional reaction by moving a lever. During more negative affect, they showed greater alpha desynchronization (activation) over the right-frontal lobe, and during a more positive affective state they showed relatively greater left-frontal activation. These frontal lobe effects may not be characteristic of the whole hemisphere: Davidson (1984) has found that right parietal activation seems to increase as subjects view both positive and negative emotional material.

A particularly relevant finding for understanding the neuropsychology of depression was that subjects scoring high on the Beck Depression Inventory showed increased right-frontal EEG activation during a baseline recording, when no emotional manipulation had been undertaken (Schaffer et al. 1983). In addition, other assessments with these depressed subjects showed them to perform poorly on visuospatial tasks, consistent with the notion of a frontal inhibition of posterior right-hemisphere representative functions in depression. Davidson (Chapter 1) has proposed that there is a reciprocity between anterior and posterior regions within each hemisphere that must be considered in explaining hemispheric roles in emotion.

The need to consider differential anterior and posterior influences has also become important in interpreting the effects of brain lesions on emotional orientation. Robinson and Starkstein (Chapter 2) have observed emotional changes after stroke that are generally consistent with the lesion effects described by Gainotti (1972), but only if the lesion is in the frontal region. In fact, the degree of reported depression after stroke increases as the lesion approaches the frontal pole of the left hemisphere, but decreases as the lesion approaches the frontal pole of the right hemisphere. At least one interpretation of these effects is that the frontal lesion disinhibits the hemisphere's characteristic affective orientation.

Finset's observations of emotional effects of lesions seem to confirm the findings of Robinson et al. Finset (1983; also see Chapter 3) has formulated a quadrant model, in which a balance in emotional functioning must be struck through both inter- and intrahemispheric relations.

It has often been observed that frontal lesions produce a "disinhibition syndrome," in which the patient shows poor impulse control. Luria (1973) observed that such personality changes were more frequent after right- than left-hemisphere lesions. Differentiating frontal from more posterior hemispheric function may thus prove essential, and may lead to a more specific neuropsychological model than the notion of "hemispheric" activation in a certain emotion. As soon as frontal-lobe function is considered, however, it becomes clear that differentiating among its functional regions could prove instructive; there are several indications of major differences in psychological roles of orbital and dorsolateral regions of frontal cortex (see Flor-Henry 1977).

If further research confirms the hypothesis that the right-frontal lobe inhibits right-posterior representative functions in depression, the theoretical challenge becomes understanding the functional significance of this intrahemispheric interaction. Could depression serve the adaptive function of allowing the organism to conserve its resources when its coping efforts have failed? Does the frontal lobe inhibit the affectively responsive right-posterior regions as part of this conservation strategy?

In a similar vein, we might speculate that the control of the right hemisphere's functioning by frontal inhibition is an important part of affective self-regulation in normal personality. With right-frontal lesions, patients may show a disinhibition of impulses and social inappropriateness. Does this suggest that in a neurologically intact brain we might find inadequate right-frontal self-modulation in a personality disorder such as psychopathy?

An important model for anterior-posterior dynamics within a hemisphere may be the interaction between expressive and receptive language systems of the left hemisphere. Although most often studied in terms of cognitive function, these regions may be important to affective self-regulation as well. Consistent with the findings of Robinson et al., it is the Broca's aphasic, with an anterior left-hemisphere lesion and expressive language deficits, who shows frustration and dysphoria (Benson and Geschwind 1975). In contrast, patients with damage to Wernicke's area, who have a language comprehension deficit, may show inappropriately positive affect. In addition to demonstrating how intrahemispheric relations may be important to affective orientation, the observations with these patients may suggest how the roles of anterior and posterior left-hemisphere regions in speech control might reflect more general roles of these regions in self-control.

The Broca's aphasic can produce few words, but the words the patient does produce are often highly meaningful—as if the posterior language comprehension regions are providing substantial on-line monitoring of the potential productions. In contrast, the Wernicke's aphasic may show a kind of disinhibition of language production. The patient may exhibit "jargon aphasia," in which speech is fluent but meaningless, as if the posterior self-monitoring functions are essential for organizing coherent speech.

Does the inappropriate positive affect of the Wernicke's aphasic suggest a loss of critical self-monitoring not just in language production but in psychological functioning generally? Kolb and Milner (1981) found that executing complex motor acts requires an intact left-parietal region, as if the perceptual monitoring by that region is used as a target to guide the appropriate actions. Together with the speech effects, these observations may suggest a general role of left-posterior regions in self-monitoring. Does the dysphoria of the Broca's aphasic suggest an exaggeration of this posterior self-monitoring? Highly anxious persons may show an exaggeration of left-hemisphere processing (Tucker et al. 1978; Tyler and Tucker 1982). Is normal anxiety associated with an exaggeration of critical self-evaluation from posterior left-hemisphere regions?

In clinical settings, depression and anxiety are often found together. But it may be important to differentiate between these affects to clarify the neuropsychological mechanisms of emotion. For example, when Perris et al. (1978) related left- and right-hemisphere EEG data to specific symptoms of psychiatric patients, it was frontal EEG activity that appeared most predictive, with a differential influence from left and right frontal regions. Left-frontal activity covaried more with ideational rumination and symptoms suggesting anxiety, whereas right-frontal activity covaried more with the degree of mood disorder. Is the affective orientation of the patient with an anterior left-hemisphere lesion best described as depressed or anxious?

Some specifications of these emotional dimensions may be necessary for further theoretical progress. Given the intrahemispheric mechanisms in affective self-regulation on both left and right sides, a "negative" emotional reaction could result from a cascading effect of imbalance to any of several regions. Through carefully examining the nature of a patient's emotional response and relating it to the cognitive operations of specific cortical regions, it may be possible to develop a neuropsychology that describes not only mechanisms of perception and cognition but of personality.

AFFECTIVE CONTROL OF COGNITION: LIMBIC MECHANISMS?

Although the actual functions of any of these several cortical regions remain to be determined, this account of emotional self-regulation in terms of cortical systems is still something of a top-down model. The bias in neuropsychology to emphasize cortical mechanisms—what Wood (1985) has termed cortical chauvinism—seems similar to the bias in psychological theories of emotion to emphasize higher, cognitive processes.

It may also be important to consider mechanisms through which more primitive affective systems regulate cognition. There have been important suggestions of affective control of cognitive function in the depression literature. Furthermore, psychometric studies with normal persons suggest there may be a specificity of this affective control, whereby certain kinds emotional arousal are most influential in the cognitive domain. In this section, I will review evidence of affective control of cognition both in clinical depression research and in normal psychometric studies. I will then describe a theoretical model that proposes that affective processes prime specific aspects of attention and cognition. Finally, I will consider the possibility that the limbic system mechanisms that regulate memory and cognition exert this regulation as a function of the organism's adaptive concerns.

We have seen that the impairment of right-hemisphere performance capacity in a depressed mood may normalize when mood improves (Brumback et al. 1980; Kronfol et al. 1978). Although some of the negative cognitive processing characteristics of depressed persons are probably trait-like, there are also suggestions that a negative cognitive bias may not be observed unless the person is currently depressed. Lewinsohn et al. (1981) followed a large sample of persons, some of whom became depressed. Although during the depressive episodes the subjects showed the negative cognitive bias reported in other research, a review of the previous assessments with these patients showed no such bias during their previous euthymic state.

Although some studies fail to find cognitive effects of mood variation in normal persons, there have been reports that an induced depressive affect can result in a negative bias in cognition and memory in normal persons. In reviewing this literature, Isen (1984) suggests that mood induction effects are often weak because normal subjects resist a depressed mood with active coping strategies. She finds, however, that experimental manipulation of positive affect reliably produces a positive bias in cognitive processing and in memory access. Although for clinical applications the negative cognitive bias with depressed affect is most important, from a theoretical vantage the findings with positive affect are equally important in indicating that a person's emotional state may exert a causal influence on cognitive processing.

In current research on emotion and memory, the influence of emotion on memory is described through a strictly cognitive theory, without any reference to emotional processes that are separate from the cognitive system. Bower (1981), for example, proposes that emotion is an informational cue like any other cue, and when it has been associated with a given memory it may later serve as a retrieval cue to facilitate access to that memory. Thus we can remember positive experiences when in a positive mood because the positive mood was associated with those experiences at the time of encoding, and when present at retrieval the positive mood facilitates access to the experiences.

However, this formulation of emotional influences wholly in terms of cognitive mechanisms does not seem to fit a neuropsychological model. Rather than one undifferentiated cognitive representational network, in which an emotion is just one more informational node, the brain evidences a hierarchic organization, in which the most elementary functional systems are responsive to adaptive needs, and higher cognitive representational abilities are elaborated from these more elementary systems. In addition, important emotional processes seem to go on in parallel to the cognitive representational processes of the cortex. For example, Mesulam (1981) describes experiments in which monkeys were presented with various stimuli as the brain regions supporting their attentional orientation to these stimuli were examined with single-unit recording. Cells in parietal cortex seemed to track the spatial location of the stimuli. There were also cells in cingulate cortex, the paleocortex of the limbic system, that showed responses—but only when the stimulus had adaptive significance for the animal. The limbic regions thus seemed to provide an adaptive monitoring function to direct attentional capacity according to motivational and emotional factors.

This is a time of rapid progress in the neuropsychology of memory. Neuropsychologists are using cognitive-psychology concepts and methods to clarify the nature of limbic contributions to memory processes; cognitive psychologists are making extensive use of the neuropsychological evidence (see, for example, Squire 1986). So far, little attention has been paid to questions of the emotional constraints that we might expect to operate on the limbic control of memory and cognition. But if we do consider how the emotional functions of limbic structures might figure in the control of memory by these structures, it would seem that emotional influences may operate not as additional information nodes in semantic networks, but as external and parallel control processes. The neuropsychological model of memory mechanisms is still rather inarticulate, but it does seem as if long-term storage—the cognitive representational network—occurs at the cortical level in the structures that are involved in the initial perceptual processing of the data. However, with the exception of memory for routinized motor programs, it also appears that limbic structures are essential for the formation of memories (Squire 1986). Thus, the limbic structures appear to select some of the data for maintenance in working memory, thus increasing the probability of long-term cortical storage. From an evolutionary perspective, it seems more than a coincidence that the brain's allocation of its limited memory capacity occurs in structures with elementary emotional and motivational functions. Emotions may not be just more bits of data in the associational machine—they may be the engines of thought.

If the limbic system exerts primitive adaptive controls on memory, these would operate in parallel to the cortical representational network. Rather than influencing just the informational nodes with which it is associated, an emotional state may exert broad and pervasive influences on all memory access.

Some recent findings on cognitive effects of emotional arousal may be relevant. Johnson and Tversky (1983) induced a negative emotional response in subjects by having them read a story about a violent crime. In a supposedly separate experiment, they then asked the subjects to rate the expected likelihood of a variety of events, predicting that other kinds of violent crime would be perceived more likely, given the "spread" of semantic activation to cognitive elements related to the story. What they found, however, was a nonspecific increase in expected frequency of all negative life events, whether or not they were related to violent crimes. The implication may be that affective influences may not operate in the same way as informational cues in the cognitive representational system, but may exert a more pervasive and global influence, in parallel to representational mechanisms.

With the possible exception of psychoanalysis, psychological theories of emotion have had little to say about this kind of bottom-up influence, whereby elementary emotional processes produce changes in cognition. There have been findings from factor-analytic studies, however, that may be relevant to this kind of bottom-up influence.

Unlike the categorical theories of emotion, which have attempted to enumerate the fundamental emotions, the factor-analytic studies have searched for the essential dimensions along which human emotions vary. A consistent finding has been that two factors seem to underlie subjects' self-ratings of emotions. These have most often been described as a pleasantness-unpleasantness factor and an arousal or intensity factor. The various categories of emotion can then be described in terms of these two factors. However, Tellegen (1985) has recently argued that an equally valid rotation of these factors (at 45 degrees to the conventional solution) would describe two emotional dimensions, each of which increases in intensity: a Positive Affect factor, ranging from sluggish to elated, and a Negative Affect factor, ranging from calm to anxious and hostile.

This characterization of emotional dimensions may be helpful for researching the emotions found in clinical settings. Tellegen's Positive Affect factor may describe the depression-elation dimension, whereas his Negative Affect factor may describe a relaxation-anxiety dimension. Although this formulation is an elaboration on the factors described in Tellegen's questionnaire studies, there are some indications that this extension to clinically relevant affective dimensions may be valid. Watson and Tellegen (1985) report, for example, that depressed patients are characterized more by their low score for the Positive Affect factor than by a high score for the Negative Affect factor.

If there is an essential dimensionality to emotional arousal, a specific assessment of these dimensions may be important in researching the emotional functioning of brain systems. Furthermore, it may be important that these fundamental dimensions seem to underlie subjects' choices of emotion ratings on a variety of questionnaires. Perhaps the finding itself suggests that elementary affective processes are exerting an organizing influence on the structure of the subjects' semantic processes.

To formulate a heuristic model for this kind of affective priming of cognitive representations that would account for the specificity observed by Tellegen in his factor-analytic studies, Vannatta, Rothlind, and I proposed that the depression-elation dimension of affective arousal "primes" access to hedonically positive events in memory (Tucker et al. 1986). In addition, we suggested that the relaxation-anxiety dimension primes access to threatening or aversive events specifically. Although expressed in psychological terms, this model reflects the kind of parallel adaptive controls on memory that we think might occur in limbic structures.

The prediction of this model is that a person's current emotional state will condition the appraisal of life events in specific ways.

Depression in a pure form (not including anxiety) would be expected to decrease the hedonic value and expected likelihood of positive events, but it may not increase the expectancy of negative events. Anxiety or hostility, on the other hand, would be expected to increase the expectancy of threatening events more than it would decrease the expectancy of rewarding events.

There have been findings of emotion-cognition interaction that are consistent with this formulation of primitive priming. Isen (1984) reviews research by Nasby and Yando (1982) that showed that a happy mood facilitated children's learning of positive-trait adjectives. However, a sad mood did not facilitate the learning of negative-trait adjectives, but rather impaired the learning of positive ones. This specificity of emotional influence could be seen as consistent with the depression-elation modulating hedonically positive memory access. McLeod et al. (1986) presented threatening words on a display screen during an attentional task. Anxious but not normal subjects showed performance impairment when the target was near the threatening words, as if their attention were attracted to the words. Importantly, depressed subjects did not show this effect. Again, this could be taken as support for the notion that it is anxiety or hostility that primes negative cognition, whereas depression decrements the priming of positive cognition.

Vannatta (1986) tested the predictions of the primitive adaptive priming model by assessing subjects' current emotional state according to Tellegen's two dimensions and then having them rate the expected likelihood and the subjective impact of both major and minor threatening and rewarding life events. Although not all ratings showed significant correlations with current mood state, the correlations that were obtained were consistent with the predicted specificity of primitive adaptive priming. For major life events, higher current positive affect (elation) predicted greater expected likelihood of rewards but was unrelated to expectancy of threatening events. For minor life events, higher negative affect (anxiety/hostility) predicted a greater rated impact of threatening events but did not influence the expectancy of rewards.

SELF-REGULATION THROUGH ACTIVATION AND AROUSAL

There may be a more fundamental level at which depressive affect operates in the brain. The depression-elation dimension and the relaxation-anxiety dimension may both be integral to the brain's self-regulation of arousal and elementary attentional structure.

Thayer (1978) used factor analysis to develop a scale for subjects to use in reporting their current level of physiological activation. He found two factors to emerge from these self-reports. One dimension of activation varies from calm to tense and nervous; another varies from sleepy, tired, and drowsy to lively, full of pep, and energetic. Another dimension varies from restful, quiescent, and calm, to jittery, fearful, and clutched up. Are these two factors of activation further reflections of the depression-elation and relaxation-anxiety dimensions that are suggested by Tellegen's (1985) model of emotion?

To attempt to understand the relation between affective arousal mechanisms and neuropsychological arousal mechanisms, Williamson and I examined the literature on the neurotransmitter pathways that have been implicated as important to psychiatric disorders (Tucker and Williamson 1984). There were several indications that these neurotransmitter pathways, although bilaterally distributed, may be differentially important to the left and right hemispheres. These neural mechanisms seem to produce changes in affective state and attentional function simultaneously; at this neuropsychological level the distinction between attention and affect becomes remarkably fuzzy. Perhaps the most important conclusion to be drawn from this literature is that the brain's controls on its arousal and attention are qualitatively specific. It is not the case that brain arousal is increased in a quantitative fashion; rather, the mechanisms that turn the brain on alter its function qualitatively.

Several neurotransmitter pathways are important to regulating neural activity. Williamson and I focused on the dopamine and norepinephrine systems that seem to play primary roles in augmenting brain function. Understanding the qualitative changes in brain activity produced by these systems proved difficult. We found the theoretical model of Pribram and McGuinness (1975) to be helpful in suggesting ways that brain systems self-regulate their levels of activity. Pribram and McGuinness (1975) differentiated between a tonic activation system that supports motor readiness and a phasic arousal system that supports perceptual orienting. Williamson and I found that this framework helped explain many of the features of dopaminergic and noradrenergic function.

The dopamine pathways appear to be integral to motor readiness. But they do not simply increase the quantity of motor behavior. Rather with high levels of dopaminergic function such as produced by certain drugs, animal show a restricted range of behavior; a few actions are performed repeatedly. With even higher levels of dopaminergic modulation of brain function, the animals exhibit routinized and stereotyped behavior. The tonic activation produced by the motor readiness system seems to afford a qualitative control mechanism, rather than a simple increase in the quantity of brain activity.

The norepinephrine pathways are particularly interesting for present purposes, since the catecholamine hypothesis of the affective disorders suggests they are dysfunctional in depression (Schildkraut 1965), and pharmacological treatment of depression is often thought to augment norepinephrine function. These pathways target widespread brain regions, including a particularly dense innervation of cingulate cortex. Because norepinephrine depletion in animal research impairs habituation mechanisms, we proposed that this pathway is integral to the phasic arousal system described by Pribram and McGuinness. The positive effect of a noradrenergically mediated increase in habituation through repetition is a facilitation of the brain's responsiveness to novelty. This novelty facilitation may be integral to neural mechanisms of attentional orienting.

Williamson and I theorized that these different ways of augmenting neural activity may underlie the attentional processes of the left and right hemispheres. Yet the more fundamental differentiation of these systems is between front and back: the tonic motor readiness system supports anterior motor organization, while the phasic arousal system supports the perceptual orienting of posterior regions. A kind of alignment of left/right with front/back suggested by hemispheric specialization for these attentional control modes is consistent with substantial evidence that the left hemisphere handles complex motor coordination, whereas the right hemisphere deals with integration of bilateral perceptual data. The constancy of the tonic dopaminergic activation system may be important to controlling not only routinized motor sequences but the left hemisphere's analytic cognition. The novelty selection by the phasic noradrenergic arousal system may support not only the participatory attentional mode of posterior cortex, but the right hemisphere's holistic conceptual skills.

This theoretical formulation of the attentional controls underlying hemispheric cognitive skills assumes that there is a limited capacity to working memory. It then considers the effects of the tonic and phasic attentional controls on the allocation of memory capacity. The constancy or redundancy bias of the tonic activation system retains only a few elements in working memory. With a high degree of influence from this control mechanism, attention becomes highly focused: there is a thorough cognitive representation of a few elements. In contrast, when the habituation or novelty bias of the phasic arousal system is more influential, the organism orients to many novel data. Working memory is soon saturated with a broad range of unique elements, producing an expansive attentional scope.

In the temporal domain, considering the rate of change in information processing over time, the redundancy or constancy bias leads to a "tight" form of change control. With a bias against change, the changes that do occur will be highly determined by the semantics of the cognitive system; the elementary cybernetics of the tonic activation system may thus support the left hemisphere's sequential cognitive processing. With the more "loose" change control that results from modulation of attention by the phasic arousal system, there may be greater support for the right hemisphere's imaginative flexibility.

If these speculations are correct, it may be possible to understand how the more complex cognitive operations of the two hemispheres have emerged to capitalize on the control features of more elementary self-regulatory mechanisms. And these mechanisms are as much affective as they are attentional. When norepinephrine pathways are stimulated with drugs such as cocaine (Cooper et al. 1974), the result is not only an expansive attention but the subjective experience of elation. Evidence suggesting that norepinephrine pathways are right-lateralized comes from several sources. Pearlson and Robinson (1981) found that lesions of right- but not left-frontal lobe in rats decreased norepinephrine bilaterally. Assays of norepinephrine in human thalamus show it is higher on the right in the majority of regions (Oke et al. 1978).

Serotonin pathways are also thought to be important to depression, and to the therapeutic effect of antidepressant drugs. There have been several suggestions of asymmetric function of these pathways as well. Sai-Halasz et al. (1958) gave normal subjects dimethyltryptamine (DMT), thought to achieve its hallucinogenic effects through altering serotonin pathways, and observed neurologic soft signs on the left side of the body. Gottfries et al. (1974) measured 5-hydroxyindolacetic acid, a serotonin metabolite, in the cerebrospinal fluid of psychiatric patients and found it to correlate with right-hemisphere, but not left-hemisphere, event-related brain potentials. Mandell and Knapp (1979) found serotonin to be asymmetric in mice brains. Giving the mice cocaine increased this asymmetry, while giving them lithium decreased it.

Lithium is used to control the uncontrolled elation of manics. When it is administered to normal subjects, it has been found to produce EEG slowing that is greatest in the right parietal region (Flor-Henry 1979). Some manic patients complain that lithium impairs their creativity (Schou 1979). Interestingly, there seems to be a high incidence of affective disorders among creative artists (Andreasen and Powers 1975). Recently, Shaw et al. (1986), used a double-blind experiment to examine whether discontinuing lithium for manic patients would improve creative thinking; scores on a remote associates tests improved while the patients were off lithium, then decreased again with resumption of lithium. These findings may be consistent with the formulation that the expansive attentional scope produced by the phasic arousal system is integral to an elated mood.

It is perhaps easiest to understand the pathological extremes of the attentional effects of these affective dimensions. The constancy bias that occurs when the tonic activation system is engaged by anxiety or hostility can be seen as producing the motor and ideational stereotypies of the obsessive-compulsive at one level, and perhaps the fragmented attention of the schizophrenic at another. This constancy bias might be described as producing excessive "parsing" of the person's cognition (Pribram and McGuinness 1975), such that fixation on a given set of cognitive elements precludes integration across semantic domains. The grandiosity and volatile attention of the manic may reflect a pathological degree of modulation by the phasic arousal system. This kind of control could be seen as excessive "chunking," such that the manic's concepts integrate across semantic domains even when this becomes nonsensical. Although perhaps best illustrated in their extreme forms, these controls may also be integral to normal attention. An unexpected implication of this theoretical model is that optimal as well as pathological self-regulation of attentional function is accomplished through neural systems that are inherently affective. To focus attention and achieve consistency in mental operations over time may be impossible without an adequate level of anxiety. To achieve an expansive attentional scope and get the "big picture," one may need to muster up an adequate level of elation.

Experimental manipulation of positive affect supports this model of structural changes in attention with increased elation. Isen (1984) reports that subjects in whom positive affect had been induced by an experience of success or by receipt of a small gift showed a preference for a loosely structured rather than methodical approach to a problem-solving task. Positive affect also improved subjects' access to remote associations—a conventional test of creativity. For a problem-solving task that required a novel, creative approach for solution, induction of positive affect produced a significant facilitation of performance (Isen 1984).

Thus when considering the close relationships among affect, arousal, and attention we find another perspective on the cerebral representation of depressed affect. Depression seems to involve a decreased functioning of a neural system that regulates elementary aspects of attentional function. In many ways this is a primitive level of brain function. The norepinephrine pathways that seem to form the major component of the phasic arousal system have their origins in the locus ceruleus of the brain stem. And at this primitive level, depression is a simple enough mechanism to be manipulated by drugs, for example, those that alter the neurochemistry of the norepinephrine pathways.

Yet we have also seen suggestions that this primitive control mechanism is integral to some of the most complex aspects of human creative intelligence. There may be important relations of this primitive cerebral mechanism of depression with each of the higher brain systems we have considered. Consider the dense noradrenergic innervation of cingulate cortex (Bloom 1978); does this suggest that the hedonic monitoring function of the limbic system (Mesulam 1981) is accomplished in part through engaging the noradrenergic phasic arousal mechanism? The norepinephrine pathways enter the cortex at the frontal pole, then course back throughout the cortex; does the frontal lobe, especially on the right, have some role in regulating this noradrenergic modulation of posterior cortex? Can a disruption of these pathways help explain some of the frontal-lesion effects in humans? If it is correct that the right hemisphere's cognitive skills are dependent on the expansive attentional orientation of the phasic arousal system, does this suggest, then, the mechanism for the poor right-hemisphere performance of depressives?

CONCLUSION

It seems likely that depressive affect will be found not in one place in the brain, but many. Although this distribution of affective control mechanisms at multiple levels of brain organization causes difficulty for any simple notions of the biology of depression, it also causes the study of depressed affect to be more than the study of an isolated disease process. To provide a satisfactory characterization of the cerebral representation of depressive affect, we may need to develop a general understanding of the neural mechanisms of adaptive, affective self-regulation.

REFERENCES

Abramson LY, Seligman MEP, Teasdale JD: Learned helplessness in humans: critique and reformulation. J Abnorm Psychol 87:49–74, 1978

Andreasen NJC, Powers PS: Creativity and psychosis: an examination of conceptual style. Arch Gen Psychiatry 32:70–73, 1975

Bear DM: Hemispheric specialization and the neurology of emotion. Arch Neurology 40:195–202, 1983

Bear DM, Fedio P: Quantitative analysis of interictal behavior in temporal lobe epilepsy. Arch Neurology 34:454–467, 1977

Beck AT, Rush AJ, Shaw BF, et al: Cognitive therapy of depression. New York, Guilford Press, 1979

Benson DF, Geschwind N: The aphasias and related disturbances, in Clinical Neurology. Edited by Baker AB, Baker LD. New York, Harper and Row, 1975

Best CT: Hemispheric asymmetries in the perception and expression of infant facial emotions. Paper presented at the meeting of the International Neuropsychological Society. Denver, CO, 1986

Bloom FE: Central noradrenergic systems: physiology and pharmacology. Psychopharmacology: a generation of progress, 1978, pp. 131–141

Borod JC, Koff E, Buck R: The neuropsychology of facial expression: data from normal and brain-damaged adults, in Noverbal Communication in the Clinical Context. Edited by Blanck P, Buck R, Rosenthal R. University Park, PA, Penn State Press, 1986

Bower GH: Mood and memory. Am Psychol 36:129–148, 1981

Brumback RA, Staton RD, Wilson: Neuropsychological study of children during and after remission of endogenous depressive episodes. Percept Mot Skills 50:1163–1167, 1980

Buck R: Prime theory: an integrated view of motivation and emotion. Psychol Rev 92:389–413, 1985

Buck R, Duffy J: Nonverbal communication of affect in brain-damaged patients. Cortex 16:351–362, 1980

Campbell R: Asymmetries in interpreting and expressing a posed facial expression. Cortex 14:327–342, 1978

Cannon WB: Bodily Changes in Pain, Hunger, Fear, and Rage: An Account of Recent Researches into the Function of Emotional Excitement. New York, Appleton, 1929

Cooper JR, Bloom FE, Roth RH: The Biochemical Basis of Neuropharmacology. New York, Oxford University Press, 1974

Davidson RJ: Hemispheric specialization for affective processes in normals: behavioral and electrophysiological studies. Address presented at the Society for Biological Psychiatry. Atlanta, GA, May 5, 1978

Davidson RJ: Affect, cognition, and hemispheric specialization, in Emotion, Cognition and Behavior. Edited by Izard CE, Kagan J, Zajonc R. New York, Cambridge University Press (in press)

Dopson WG, Beckwith BE, Tucker DM, et al: Asymmetry of facial expression in spontaneous emotion. Cortex 20:243–252, 1984

Ekman P, Hager JC, Friesen WV: The asymmetry of emotional and deliberate facial actions. Psychophysiology 18:101–106, 1981

Finset A: Depressive behavior, outburst crying, and emotional indifference in left hemiplegics. Paper presented at the Second Annual Symposium of Models and Techniques of Cognitive Rehabilitation. Indianapolis, IN, March 1983

Flor-Henry P: Psychosis and temporal lobe epilepsy: a controlled investigation. Epilepsia 10:363–395, 1969

Flor-Henry P: Progress and problems in psychosurgery, in Current Psychiatric Therapies. Edited by Maserman JH. New York, Grune and Stratton, 1977

Flor-Henry P: On certain aspects of the localization of cerebral systems regulating and determining emotion. Biol Psychiatry 14:677–698, 1979

Gainotti G: Studies on the functional organization of the minor hemisphere. International Journal of Mental Health 1:78–82, 1972

Galin D, Diamond R, Braff D: Lateralization of conversion symptoms: more frequent on the left. Am J Psychiatry 134:578–580, 1977

Goldstein K: The effect of brain damage on personality. Psychiatry 15:245–260, 1952

Goldstein SG, Filskov SB, Weaver LA, et al: Neuropsychological effects of electroconvulsive therapy. J Clin Psychol 33:798–806, 1977

Gottfries CG, Perris C, Roos BE: Visual averaged evoked responses (AER) and monoamine metabolites in cerebrospinal fluid (CSF). Acta Psychiatr Scand 255:135–142, 1974

Gruzelier JH: Individual differences in dynamic process asymmetries in the normal and pathological brain, in Individual Differences in Hemispheric Specialization. Edited by Glass A. New York, Plenum Press, 1986

Hall MM, Hall GC, Lavoie P: Ideation in patients with unilateral or bilateral midline brain lesions. J Abnorm Psychol 73:526–531, 1986

Isen AM: Toward understanding the role of affect in cognition, in Handbook of Social Cognition, Vol. 3. Edited by Wyer RS, Jr., Srull TK. Hillsdale, NJ, Erlbaum, 1984

James W: What is emotion? Mind 4:118–204, 1884

Johnson EJ, Tversky AT: Affect, generalization and the perception of risk. J Pers Soc Psychol 45:20–31, 1983

Kenyon FE: Hypochondriasis: a clinical study. Br J Psychiatry 110:478–488, 1964

Kinsbourne M, Bemporad B: Lateralization of emotion: a model and the evidence, in The Psychobiology of Affective Development. Edited by Fox N, Davidson RJ. Hillsdale, NJ, Erlbaum, (in press)

Kolb B, Milner B: Performance of complex arm and facial movements after focal brain lesions. Neuropsychologia 19:491–503, 1981

Kolb B, Taylor L: Neocortical mechanisms of emotional behavior. Paper presented to the University of Chicago Symposium on Psychological and Biological Processes in the Development of Emotion. Chicago, IL, August 1986

Kronfol Z, Hamsher K, Digre K, et al: Depression and hemisphere functions: changes associated with unilateral ECT. Br J Psychiatry 132:560–567, 1978

Ladavas E, Nicoletti R, Rizzolatti G, et al: Right hemisphere interference during negative affect: a reaction time study. Neuropsychologia 22:479–485, 1984

Lazarus R: Thoughts on the relations between emotion and cognition. Am Psychol 37:1019–1024, 1982

Lazarus R: Constructs of the mind in adaptation. Paper presented to the University of Chicago Symposium on Psychological and Biological Processes in the Development of Emotion. Chicago, IL, August 1986

Leventhal H, Tomarken AJ: Emotion: today's problems. Ann Rev Psychol 37:565–610, 1986

Levy J: Individual difference in cerebral hemisphere asymmetry: theoretical issues and experimental considerations, in Cerebral Hemisphere Asymmetry: Method, Theory, and Application. Edited by Hellige J. Praeger, New York, 1982

Levy J, Haller W, Banich MT, et al: Are variations among right-handed individuals in perceptual asymmetries caused by characteristic arousal differences between hemispheres? J Exp Psychol [Hum Percept] 9:329–358, 1983

Lewinsohn PM, Steinmetz JL, Larson DW, et al: Depression-related cognitions: antecedent or consequence? J Abnorm Psychol 90:213–219, 1981

Ley RG, Bryden MP: Hemispheric differences in processing emotions and faces. Brain Lang 7:127–138, 1979

Liotti M, Sava D, Caffarra P, et al: Hemispheric differences in patients affected by depression and anxiety (manuscript in preparation)

Luria AR: The Working Brain: An Introduction to Neuropsychology. New York, Basic Books, 1973

MacLeod C, Mathews A, Tata A: Attentional bias in emotional disorders. J Abnorm Psychol 95:15–20, 1986

Mandell AJ, Knapp S: Asymmetry and mood, emergent properties of serotonin regulation. Arch Gen Psychiatry 36:909–916, 1979

Mandler G: Mind and Body: Psychology of Emotion and Stress. New York, WW Norton, 1985

Mesulam MM: A cortical network for directed attention and unilateral neglect. Ann Neurol 10:309–325, 1981

Monrad-Krohn GH: On the dissociation of voluntary and emotional innervation in facial paresis of central origin. Brain 47:22–35, 1924

Nauta WJH: The problem of the frontal lobe: a reinterpretation. J Psychiatr Res 8:167–187, 1971

Oke A, Keller R, Meffort I, et al: Lateralization of norepinephrine in human thalamus. Science 200:1141–1143, 1978

Pearlson GD, Robinson RG: Suction lesions of the frontal cerebral cortex in the rat induced asymmetrical behavioral and catecholaminergic responses. Brain Res 218:233–242, 1981

Perris C: Averaged evoked responses (AFR) in patients with affective disorders. Acta Psychiatr Scand [Suppl] 255, 1974

Perris C: EEG techniques in the measurement of the severity of depressive syndromes. Neuropsychobiology 1:16–25, 1975

Perris C, Monakhov K, Von Knorring L, et al: Systemic structural analysis of the EEG of depressed patients. Neuropsychobiology 4:207–228, 1978

Pribram KH: Emotions, in Handbook of Clinical Neuropsychology. Edited by Filskov SK, Boll TJ. New York, Wiley-Interscience, 1981

Pribram KH, McGuinness D: Arousal, activation, and effort in the control of attention. Psychol Rev 82:116–149, 1975

Roland PE: Metabolic measures of the working frontal cortex in man. Trends Neurosci 430–435, 1984

Ross E, Mesulam MM: Dominant language functions of the right hemisphere? Prosody and emotional gesturing. Arch Neurology 36:144–148, 1979

Rothbart MK, Taylor SB, Tucker DM: Facial expressions of emotion in infants: more intense on the right side of the face (manuscript in preparation)

Sackeim HA, Gur RC, Saucy MC: Emotions are expressed more intensely on the left side of the face. Science 202:434–436, 1978

Sackeim HA, Greenberg MS, Weiman AL, et al: Hemispheric asymmetry in the expression of positive and negative emotions: neurologic evidence. Arch Neurology 39:210–218, 1982

Safer MA, Leventhal H: Ear differences in evaluating emotional tone of voice and verbal content. J Exp Psychol. [Hum Percept] 3:75–82, 1977

Sai-Halasz A, Brunecker G, Szara S: Dimethyltryptamin: Ein Neues Psychoticum. Psychiatr Neurol (Basel) 135:285, 1958

Schacter F, Singer JE: Cognitive social and psychological determinants of emotional states. Psychol Rev 69:379–399, 1962

Schaffer CE, Davidson RJ, Saron C: Frontal and parietal electroencephalogram asymmetry in depressed and nondepressed subjects. Biol Psychiatry 18:753–762, 1983

Schildkraut J: The catecholamine hypothesis of affective disorders: a review of supporting evidence. Am J Psychiatry 122:509–522, 1965

Schou M: Artistic productivity and lithium prophylaxis in manic-depressive illness. Br J Psychiatry 135:97–103, 1979

Shapiro D: Neurotic Styles. New York, Basic Books, 1965

Shaw ED, Mann JJ, Stokes PE, et al: Effects of lithium carbonate on associative productivity and idiosyncracy in bipolar outpatients. Am J Psychiatry 143:1166–1169, 1986

Squire LR: Mechanisms of memory. Science 232:1612–1619, 1986

Swenson RA, Tucker DM: Lateralized cognitive style and self-description. Int J Neurosci 21:91–100, 1983

Tellegen A: Structures of mood and personality and their relevance to assessing anxiety, with an emphasis on self-report, in Anxiety and the Anxiety Disorders. Edited by Tuma AH, Maser JD. Hillsdale, NJ, Erlbaum, 1985

Thayer RE: Toward a psychological theory of multidimensional activation (arousal). Motivation and Emotion 2:1–34, 1978

Tucker DM: Lateral brain function, emotion, and conceptualization. Psychol Bull 89:19–46, 1981

Tucker DM: Neural control of emotional communication, in Nonverbal Communication in the Clinical Context. Edited by Blanck P, Buck R, Rosenthal R. Cambridge, England, Cambridge University Press, 1986

Tucker DM, Newman JP: Verbal versus imaginal cognitive strategies in the inhibition of emotional arousal. Cognitive Therapy and Research 5:197–202, 1981

Tucker DM, Dawson SL: Asymmetric EEG power and coherence as method actors generated emotions. Biol Psychol 19:63–75, 1984

Tucker DM, Williamson PA: Asymmetric neural control systems in human self-regulation. Psychol Rev 91:185–215, 1984

Tucker DM, Watson RG, Heilman KM: Affective discrimination and evocation in patients with right parietal disease. Neurology 26:354, 1976

Tucker DM, Antes JR, Stenslie CE, et al: Anxiety and lateral cerebral function. J Abnorm Psychol 87:380–383, 1978

Tucker DM, Vannatta K, Rothlind J: Activation and arousal systems and primitive controls on cognitive priming. Paper presented to the University of Chicago Symposium on Psychological and Biological Processes in the Development of Emotion. Chicago, IL, August 1986

Tyler SK, Tucker DM: Anxiety and perceptual structure: individual differences in neuropsychological function. J Abnorm Psychol 91:210–220, 1982

Vannatta K: Emotions and expectations of positive and negative experiences. University of Oregon, 1986 (unpublished study)

Von Knorring L: Interhemispheric EEG differences in affective disorders, in Laterality and Psychopathology. Edited by Flor-Henry P, Gruzelier J. Amsterdam, Elsevier, 1983

Watson D, Tellegen A: Toward a consensual structure of mood. Psychol Bull 98:219–235, 1985

Wood F: Personal communication, 1985

Chapter 7

Hemisphere Interactions in Depression

Marcel Kinsbourne, M.D.

Chapter 7

Hemisphere Interactions in Depression

UNSTABLE CONTROL SYSTEMS AND PSYCHOPATHOLOGY

Contrasting explanations of psychopathology emphasize abnormal mental states induced by dynamic factors and abnormal brain states induced by endogenous chemical factors. It has become increasingly apparent that this dichotomy is spurious and should be replaced by an interactionist viewpoint. The issue of present concern, the rapidly accumulating documentation of "cerebral dysfunction" in various forms of psychopathology, can be understood only from such a perspective. Whereas abnormal mental states are precipitated by adverse environmental events, individuals vary greatly in their vulnerability to such stresses. Whether successful coping strategies are deployed depends greatly on the extent to which brain mechanisms can reorganize their function in response to the abnormal situation, permitting the individual to formulate plans for dealing with it. In this discussion I will propose that control systems in the brain maintain a balance between alternate behavioral tendencies. When its balance is distorted by adversity, a stable control system will soon normalize. In contrast, an unstable control system will react with an exaggerated and prolonged bias, which limits the individual's ability to react flexibly to the situation. An excessive response of the brain to one aspect of the situation in vulnerable persons restricts their behavioral options and compels them to deploy a limited strategy that addresses only one aspect rather than the totality of events, generating the maladaptive behavior that is by definition psychopathological. Examples follow.

A normal response to an unexpected setback is arrest of ongoing behavior. This permits a reformulation of plans. But too complete or prolonged an arrest of ongoing behavior could amount to depression. Motivated approach is a normal adaptive response. But too rigid an approach in a state of high motivation will lead to impulsive psychopathology. Monitoring the outcome of one's actions is normal. But too rigid a criterion for the completion of a motivated activity is manifested as obsessive behavior. Emotional arousal in the face of the unexpected is normal. But lack of control of swinging emotional arousal is manifested as hysteria. I will develop a model to show how the distinctive state of cerebral processors in each of several psychopathologies might generate the classical psychiatric symptomatology. The model accounts for the pattern of cerebral dysfunction that characterizes each in terms of failure of the brain to reorganize adaptively in the face of stress. I will first discuss the probable mechanism by which cerebral control systems work and the ways in which they can malfunction, and then I will attempt to explain abnormal neuropsychological test results and deviant laterality findings from this perspective. I will then suggest how various parts of the cerebrum participate in the resolution of everyday problems and explicate several psychopathological syndromes in terms of arrests and diversions of this normally ongoing sequence of events (Kinsbourne and Bemporad 1984).

OPPONENT PROCESSORS IN CONTROL OF BEHAVIOR

The organization of behavioral control at the sensorimotor level in terms of opponent processors has been well known at least since Sherrington's (1906) classical monograph. The organism's every act represents a choice between alternative possible actions, and the direction and amplitude of each action represents a choice between possible directions and alternative levels of amplitude.

A simple illustration relates to the grasp response. Grasping with one limb involves inhibiting grasp with its crossed counterpart. The grasp itself may involve the use of certain effectors, for instance thumb and forefinger, with concurrent inhibition of others, for instance the three other fingers (in "pincer grip"). The amplitude of the grasp and its force are determined by the balance between muscle agonist and antagonist for the moving parts. Imbalance at any of these levels of organization will render the action less efficient or even useless. Thus a grasp that is insufficiently opposed will yield a flexor synergism, one that may even be extreme enough to swing the reaching limb away from the target, as in certain dystonias. Failure to inhibit movement by those digits not intended for use coarsens the grasp into a full five-finger flexion, rendering it unsuitable for fine adjustments. Antagonist failure will render the grasp maximally forceful, thus crushing a delicate target. All three of these malfunctions characterize the infant (and to a lesser extent the developing child—see Fog and Fog 1963) who is not yet able to fine-tune the appropriate excitation-inhibition balance. Conversely, too great an inhibitory influence at these levels of organization generates intrusive avoidance responses and failure of the moving parts to assume their intended position (for instance, in athetosis).

In the control of voluntary behavior at a higher level of organization, this interplay between opposing response tendencies is readily apparent in circumstances that call for decisive action before all the evidence is in, or conversely, for temporary suspension of action with delay of gratification. Flexible behavioral control makes it possible to maneuver between the extremes of maximal action and inaction, depending on one's appraisal of the total situation. Inadequate control systems will, if biased, generate one or the other of these response tendencies (hasty or hesitant action) across more situations than is adaptive. Unstable control systems will cause behavior to swing unpredictably between response extremes. Affective response also results from the balance between the tendency to suspend responding, accompanied by one of the varieties of negative affect, and to continue responding, attended by positive affect and indifference to negative consequences. Again, overdeploying the former tendency generates depressive psychopathology, whereas overdeploying the latter results in pathological indifference and denial syndromes.

The opponent processor concept of the control of adaptive behavior explains why individuals suffering from psychopathology respond in stereotyped or rigid fashion to a wide range of contingencies (deploying response types that would be adaptive for anyone if confined to a much narrower range of circumstances), and yet at times show themselves fully able to respond otherwise. An illustration is derived from the hyperactive attention-deficit (ADDH) child. Although in most circumstances ADDH children respond with hasty impulsivity and ill-sustained attention, it is generally appreciated that such children can at times deploy adequate attention. Thus, their attentional control mechanisms must be in place, only underused; that is, ADDH is a quantitative, not a qualitative, abnormality. Much psychopathology involves the overuse of basically normal response tendencies, which supplant, and thus lead to underuse of, their equally normal opponent counterparts.

LATERALITY AND SELECTION BETWEEN THE CEREBRAL HEMISPHERES

Laterality effects are generally agreed to reflect the complementary specializations of the two cerebral hemispheres. The advantage of the right ear and right visual field that characterizes right-handers when they deploy their left-hemispheric language processors for purposes of solving verbal problems (such as identifying spoken or printed verbal materials) is offset by corresponding left-sided advantage when the individual is induced by test demands to use his right lateralized spatial-relational processing facilities. In psychopathology, laterality findings are often deviant and changeable even within the same patient (see Wexler, Chapter 4). If a perpetual asymmetry is interpreted literally, in terms of the conventional structural "direct access" model, as indicating which hemisphere is specialized for the task in question, this would lead one to suppose that presumably hard-wired specializations of the cerebrum are in astonishing flux in mental disorders. To draw more reasonable conclusions from deviant laterality findings in psychopathology, we must consider the mechanisms by which structural lateral specialization for cognitive purposes engenders a bias in the performance of verbal and spatial tasks.

A dichotic ear advantage and a half-field advantage indicate that the opposite hemisphere is more engaged in the processing called for by the test. Which hemisphere is more engaged is determined by the interaction between the nature of the task and the subject's strategic choices and cognitive style. Much evidence indicates that an intervening variable between the structural hemisphere specialization and the asymmetric behavior is a lateral orienting bias that derives from activation of the hemisphere in control of ongoing behavior. This concept is important for our present purposes, because if it is so, the ear or half-field "advantage" representing selective orienting of one hemisphere affords an event-related indication of the balance of activation between the hemispheres. I will therefore briefly mention some of the evidence on which the concept relies. It is reviewed in more detail in Kinsbourne (1974).

At many levels of the bisymmetric vertebrate nervous systems, paired localized neural facilities are in horizontal opponent balance (mediated by transverse commissures). Activation of an opponent processor causes the organism to turn and orient to the opposite side of space. The highest level of these multiple paired facilities is cerebral. It involves the frontal eye fields and areas of occipital cortex. Activity of the left-frontal eye field turns head, eyes, and body to the right and that of the right-frontal eye field turns these to the left. Physiological evidence from animal studies shows that agents that activate a hemisphere as a whole contralaterally bias the animal's movements. The animal keeps turning to the opposite side ("circling"). Inactivation of a hemisphere releases the directional influence of the other unaffected hemisphere. This causes orienting or even circling toward the side of the inactivated hemisphere.

When use of a specialized part of a hemisphere is called for, it is activated by ascending pathways. This activation is not limited to the specialized hemispheric area, but, presumably on account of the network characteristic of brain organization, involves other parts of the hemisphere as well. One such incidentally activated area can be the lateral orienting control center. A direct demonstration of this activation was accomplished by Kinsbourne (1972). He showed that right-handed subjects thinking about verbal questions tend to turn their head and eyes involuntarily to the right side. The same subjects, considering spatial-relational matters, look more to the left than to the right.

In other studies Kinsbourne (1970, 1973, 1975) showed that giving subjects hemisphere-specific tasks facilitates premotor visual attentional shifts to the opposite side of space even if they maintain central fixation. In a visual laterality paradigm, such premotor attentional shifts bestow an advantage on the perception of information briefly exposed in the opposite half-field. They also help the subject selectively attend to one of two synchronized verbal messages presented simultaneously to the two ears in the dichotic listening paradigm. Activating the verbal hemisphere biases attention contralaterally (to the right in a right-hander) and this contributes to the right-half-field or right-ear advantage. It is possible to deconfound the categorical nature of the task and the selectively activated hemisphere. One gives a subject a hemispherically neutral task of pattern discrimination and by simultaneously setting a secondary hemisphere-specific task, such as imposing a verbal memory load, biases attention contralaterally. The subject preferentially perceives pattern information originating in the contralateral side of space.

The above findings all reflect the hemisphere selectively activated by virtue of task demands. It is also possible to do the opposite: by inducing lateral orienting, to determine which hemisphere takes charge of the solution of problems. The method of induced lateral orientation was introduced by Kinsbourne (1975) and has been used successfully in numerous subsequent studies. An instance is the study of Lempert and Kinsbourne (1982) in which subjects listened to phrases either with head turned right or with head turned left. Subsequently they showed better recall of this verbal material if it had been encoded in the head-turned-right condition. This outcome had been predicted on the grounds that rightward head turning would engender left-hemisphere activation, which would spread to activate other parts of the hemisphere, including the language area, thus rendering the latter a more efficient encoder of verbal information.

The above methods make it possible to monitor the balance of hemisphere activation while subjects perform tasks of affective relevance.

The concept of selective hemisphere activation (Kinsbourne 1970) is essential for making sense of laterality shifts in psychopathology. A simple structural hypothesis, faced with the frequent finding of altered perceptual asymmetry without drop in performance efficiency, has to retreat to the implausible postulate of corresponding shifts in structural specialization.

LATERALITY FOR AFFECT

An extensive literature has documented a left-half-field superiority for the discrimination of facial emotions and a left-ear superiority for the discrimination of sounds and intonations of affective significance. There is some evidence, though more contentious, that this phenomenon is restricted to negative affect, and that positive affect is, if anything, left lateralized in the brain (see Chapter 1). There is some evidence also that affective facial expression is more right than left brain controlled (Borod and Koff 1984). Schwartz et al. (1975) first demonstrated that a greater right- than left-hemisphere activation mediates the effects of negative affect. Using the lateral gaze methodology, they found that while considering emotionally laden questions, specifically ones invested with negative affect, subjects looked more to the left, whereas with neutral or positive ones they looked equally right or left or even more to the right. Further insight into how the right hemisphere incorporates processed affect into the mental life of an individual is provided by experiments like the following.

Gage and Safer (1985) gave subjects information during either of two induced moods, happy or depressed, and tested them for retention in the same or alternate state. The investigators found dependence on the emotional state: subjects better remembered information that was presented and retrieved in the same state. They found it more difficult to remember what they had been told while happy when they were sad and vice versa. But this state dependence only applied to information presented to the left visual field. In other words it was the right hemisphere that encoded information contextually in relation to the prevailing affect. The left hemisphere seemed to decontextualize the information and therefore showed no state dependence. Of course, in the intact brain information is not confined to the hemisphere of input. But the side stimulated seems to emit an orienting response indicative of selective activation, and this activation increases the control over behavior of the hemisphere's typical pattern of response. An example is the finding by Davidson et al. (1987) that affective facial stimuli are judged more positively when presented to the right than to the left visual field. A study by Grijalva (1982) supports this finding, using a different methodology. Subjects' mood was established by questionnaire before and after they were presented with a number of "somatically negative" adjectives to one or the other ear. On post-test subjects showed a more depressed mood, but only if the information had been given through the left ear. Assuming that left-ear presentation generates leftward orienting based on right-hemisphere activation, it was under circumstances that would activate the right hemisphere and permit it to take control of behavior that the mood-inducing statements were incorporated into how the person felt about himself. When the left hemisphere was more in control (during rightward orienting) those statements were not given a personal connotation. Compatible findings have been generated through the use of induced lateral orientation. In a series of experiments Drake (e.g., Drake and Bingham 1985) has demonstrated that when a subject's head is turned to the right he evaluates himself more optimistically, views pictures more positively, and is more apt to continue to adhere to an existing point of view. With head turned left, subjects are more favorably disposed toward others and more readily convinced by arguments in favor of positions that they have not previously supported. We learn from studies such as the above that the affective state in which an individual meets certain situations, and how he affectively evaluates them, is not invariant, but depends to some extent on which of the hemispheres is more in control of behavior at the time.

Attentional status influences affective state. The converse might also be the case. The left hemisphere emphasizes the individual's focus of attention. The right hemisphere is specialized to establish context for that focus (Kinsbourne 1982). If an individual is in an affective state more compatible with the specialization of one hemisphere than the other, perhaps he will also be better able to perform tasks customarily programmed by that hemisphere than by the other one.

NEUROPSYCHOLOGICAL TEST PERFORMANCE IN PSYCHOPATHOLOGY

Intelligence test performance is usually regarded as a stable characteristic of the individual and so is performance on neuropsychological tests, that is, tests designed to tap the capabilities of limited specialized areas of cerebral cortex. But we have already seen that a maneuver as apparently innocuous as turning attention to right or left can manipulate the level of performance in a verbal memory test, reflective of left-hemispheric language ability. It would therefore seem possible that if a hemisphere were activated for some unrelated reason it might perform better with respect to tasks reflecting its specialization than when not so activated. Conversely, an underactivated hemisphere would generate impaired performance of relevant tests, even if it were structurally intact.

There is some evidence that patients with depression perform relatively poorly on tests thought to tap the specialized function of the right-posterior cerebral cortex (Kronfol et al. 1978). If valid, this finding should not be regarded as a "biological marker" for impairment of the right-posterior cortex in depression, but rather as reflective of a state of relative underactivation or inhibition of that part of the hemisphere as part and parcel of the distinctive pattern of cerebral use in depressive psychopathology. In contrast, in schizophrenia, tests that make demands on left-hemispheric specialization tend to be relatively poorly done (Flor-Henry and Yeudall 1979; Yeudall and Fromm-Auch 1979). This too could reflect an abnormal hemispheric state, rather than a fixed deficiency in hemispheric processing capability. The explanation of that state may be helped by a brief discussion of another type of laterality phenomenon, that generated by interference between two concurrent activities that use neural substrate within the same part of brain.

DUAL-TASK INTERFERENCE LATERALITY PARADIGMS

A static localizationist ("modular") notion of brain organization might hold that different tasks are represented in different parts of the brain. If performed concurrently they should either not interfere or interfere only in a general way by drawing upon some common resource shared by all areas of the cerebrum. Neither of these postulates is correct. Kinsbourne and Cook (1971) had subjects repeat sentences while balancing a dowel rod on the right or left index finger. They measured how long the subjects could maintain the rod in balance before they dropped it. They found and Hicks (1975) confirmed and extended the finding that in terms of balancing time, speaking and right-arm performance interfere, whereas speaking and left-hand performance do not interfere (in adults). This was predicted based on the notion that because of the network properties of brain, patterned activation giving rise to specific performances in adjacent, presumably highly connected, areas of brain would be more likely to generate cross-talk interference than loci of patterned activation less directly connected, for instance when situated in separate hemispheres. The phenomenon of interference through hemispheric sharing has been confirmed in a large number of studies using a wide range of different designs (Kinsbourne and Hiscock 1983). It can perhaps help us understand the impairment of verbal test performance in many schizophrenics.

It has long been suspected that schizophrenics, particularly those who hallucinate voices on a chronic basis, are engaged in continual subvocal verbal activity (McGuigan 1966). Bick and Kinsbourne (in press) found evidence against the possibility that the patients were "shadowing" the voices that they heard by demonstrating that if their vocal musculature is held still, their voices cease. It appears that the patients are listening to their own inner speech and projecting it upon imagined others. It could be that continual subverbalization keeps the left hemisphere persistently activated. Continual subvocalizing might explain schizophrenics' rightward-gaze bias when pondering a variety of questions (Gur 1978). This continual subverbalization could also interfere with the schizophrenic subjects' attempts at tasks that rely upon the functional specialization of the left hemisphere, thus generating the "left hemisphere" types of neuropsychological test deficits attributed to this psychopathological group.

Work in progress tends to support this viewpoint. Wood (1987) reported left-temporal-lobe blood flow enhancement in those schizophrenics who were hallucinating. The indicated increased regional metabolism could reflect the subvocal activity. Posner (1986) found some schizophrenics to have an impairment in shifting attention to the right in response to an unexpected directional cue. On the view that such a gaze shift is attention demanding and could encounter interference from other ongoing activity in the relevant (left) hemisphere, I suggested that hallucinating schizophrenics might be the subgroup to exhibit the right-gaze impairment. A preliminary chart review by Posner lent support to this idea.

Whether the above line of reasoning is ultimately vindicated or not, it illustrates a type of mechanism that should be considered in the effort to clarify the brain basis of mental disorders beyond the uninformative statement that a certain brain area is "dysfunctional" in a certain type of psychopathology.

The above concepts have recently gained support from the work of Wood, et al. (1987), who found left-temporal increases in metabolic rate in those schizophrenic subjects who reported voices, and of Posner (1986), who found schizophrenics selectively impaired in unwarned rightward orienting.

THE COMPLEMENTARY ROLES OF THE HEMISPHERES IN ONGOING BEHAVIOR

Numerous dichotomies have been formulated in the attempt to characterize the complementary functions of the two hemispheres over and above the well-known verbal/spatial formulation, and many of these appear to have merit. However, there may be an advantage in deviating from the rather limited, prevalent, task-oriented characterization of the hemispheres toward a more biologically conceived construct involving the role of hemispheric balance in controlling ongoing activity of the organism in its customary environment. Adopting Schneirla's (1959) position that deciding between approach and withdrawal is a basic capability of any motile organism, I suggested in the early 1970s that the left hemisphere is specialized for approach functions and the right for withdrawal. This formulation makes it possible to subsume both cognitive and emotional specializations within the same general concept (Fox and Davidson 1984). I have since refined this point of view by invoking a dichotomy still more fundamental in the behavior of organisms: the distinction between *continuing ongoing behavior* and *arrest of ongoing behavior* (Pribram and McGuinness 1975).

The meaning of "strong" stimulus and "weak" stimulus becomes radically modified in organisms that learn and can no longer be taken literally. By virtue of habituation, stimuli of high physical amplitude when repeated become psychologically "weak." They no longer elicit an orienting response, and ongoing behavior continues. In contrast, unexpected stimuli of a type that the animal has learned could be adaptively significant will cause it to orient and redirect its behavior, even if they are relatively faint. We therefore adapt Schneirla's (1966) statement that "high or increasing stimulative effects arouse-interruptive processes" to read: "novel stimulative effects arouse-interruptive processes." The interruption creates the opportunity for selective exploration of the novel input. Whether overt withdrawal ensues depends on what the animal learns through exercise of the selective orienting response. Only some novel stimuli and only some outcomes discrepant with expectation are taken to represent a threat to the individual's current goals or personal integrity. The decision that appears to be fundamental to the behavioral control of the animal that can learn is this: whether to continue or to interrupt what it is doing.

Left-hemisphere specialization is not limited to verbal activities. There is conclusive evidence that the left hemisphere is also specialized for the rapid identification of familiar objects regardless of their name and for the fluent performance of familiar action sequences. The overriding theme of left-hemisphere specialization would seem to be automaticity: the performance of activities that are well learned and for which the neural "programs" have been well developed and supported by a set of subroutines to cover a variety of contingencies that may arise during the execution of the action (e.g., Kinsbourne 1982). From its posterior specialization in rapid serial decoding to its anterior specialization in formulation of plans, the left hemisphere seems to be responsible for the maintenance of ongoing behavior of a type with which the individual has familiarized himself (Goldberg and Costa 1981). Such behavior is by definition decontextualized. Fully automatic behavior relies upon a fully specified subset of environmental cues and ignores all else.

In contrast, the right hemisphere's specializations include, although they are not limited to, the detection of novel and unexpected events. In laterality paradigms it is generally the unfamiliar or illegible material that enlists the right hemisphere in the processing act (Goldberg and Costa 1981). The right hemisphere is specialized for identifying patterns that are depleted or overlaid by random interference. Its function is to extrapolate from incomplete information to a plausible and speedy conclusion. To this end it is specialized for sensitivity to context.

How then do various psychopathologies distort the specialized functioning of the two cerebral hemispheres? Experimental evidence pertaining to the neuropsychology of depression and other mental disorders derives from two main sources: brain damage releasing abnormal reactions that simulate psychopathology, and neuropsychological and laterality test findings on depressed and other psychiatric cases.

BRAIN DAMAGE AND PSYCHOPATHOLOGY

The clinical picture that results from local brain damage is not confined to loss of the activity for which the affected area is specialized. It is complicated either by compensatory reorganization of function or by disinhibition of areas normally suppressed by the lesioned area, or both.

Take as an instance the frontal stroke damage found by Starkstein and Robinson (see Chapter 2) to lead to depressive reaction and sometimes even clinically obvious depression. Due to such a lesion the patient loses the planning ability that this area contributes to the control of behavior. Thus his behavior is inconsequential, unqualified by planning for long-term goals. Given this inability to plan, the patient is now much more vulnerable to external change and his behavior and mental attitude reflect this vulnerability. It is also possible that another brain area is disinhibited and gains greater control of behavior. In the case of damage to the left-frontal lobe this disinhibited area is, depending on the theorist, 1) right-frontal lobe (e.g. Sackheim et al. 1982); 2) left-posterior cortex (e.g. Davidson, Chapter 1); 3) left subcortex (Poeck 1969). The patient is depressed a) because he cannot plan, b) because he feels helpless and hopeless because he cannot plan, and/or c) because another part of the brain that contributes negative affect has been released from inhibition.

Which of the above explanations for the left-frontal depressive reaction is correct is not yet known. Theorists by and large tend to invoke a neurologizing (disinhibition) explanation and perhaps insufficiently consider the compensatory activity. The latter type of explanation will be emphasized later in this discussion.

An interesting case in point for disinhibition is afforded by the depressive reaction reported by Terzian (1964) and Rossi and Rosadini (1967) after they administered sodium amobarbital to the left carotid artery of normal right-handed volunteers. Many of them were reported to manifest a short-lived but intense depressive/dysphoric ("catastrophic") reaction. An obvious explanation, generally adopted, is that the temporary inactivation of the left hemisphere disinhibits the right hemisphere, which is the seat of the depressive response and thus temporarily takes control of behavior. A hidden assumption in this account is that the depressive reaction takes place at the time when the left hemisphere is uniformly inactivated. In fact, the clinical accounts suggest that the depressive reaction is somewhat delayed and occurs during the period of recovery from the barbiturate. Terzian (1964) observed "the patient . . . despairs and expresses a sense of guilt, of nothingness, of indignity . . . without referring to the language disturbances overcome and to the hemiplegia just resolved and ignored." That the emotional reactions occur only when the anesthetic is wearing off, and with amounts of amytal too small to cause hemiplegia or change the electroencephalogram (EEG), discredits the general assumption that the effect derives from a disinhibited contralateral hemisphere. Instead, a transitory state of intrahemispheric imbalance seems to be implicated. Further reason to reject a simplistic interhemispheric disinhibition hypothesis derives from the report of Alema et al. (1961) that in patients with unilateral brain disease, the typical affective change results only from anesthesia of the intact hemisphere. Post-insult compensatory reorganization of the intact hemisphere suffices to abolish the potential for transitory affective reaction. Similarly, the effect is not to be found in left-handers (Rossi and Rosadini 1967), whose brain organization is known to deviate from that of right-handers. Finally, larger doses of amytal, as used by Milner (see discussion in Rossi and Rosadini 1967) do not yield negative affective states, perhaps because they exert a bilateral anesthetic effect before their influence dissipates. For all these reasons, I suspect that the hemisphere recovers unevenly and that the depressive reaction is the result of intrahemispheric imbalance. If the posterior cortex recovers before the anterior, then the patient would temporarily be in a state of intrahemispheric imbalance analogous to that of the stroke patient with left-frontal disease. It might then be disinhibition of left-posterior cortex, that is, intrahemispheric disinhibition, that generates the negative effect.

When a lateralized lesion involves both anterior and posterior cerebral territory, which affective reaction type supervenes? In his pioneering study, Gainotti (1969) found right-hemispheric-damaged patients often to be inappropriately bland or even euphoric. According to Kolb and Whishaw (1980) left-frontal lesions yield pseudodepression and right-frontal lesions result in pseudopsychopathology (terminology of Blumer and Benson 1975). Robinson and Szetela (1981) have confirmed that with extensive right-sided insults the indifference reaction supervenes. Extensive left-sided disease seems to favor depressive reactions (see Chapter 2). Apparently the frontal deficit reaction predominates. In depression, an electrophysiological study produced suggestive evidence of a similar dichotomy between right- and left-frontal activity (Perris et al. 1978). This suggests, in accord with our model, that the affective reactions of posterior origin represent distortions of informational input that impact the individual's affective state indirectly, by virtue of their influence on frontal-lobe mechanisms. The attribution "frontal lobe" will have to be qualified in terms of the relevant subarea within this massive structure. At the very least, one must distinguish between orbital and dorsolateral lesions, selective damage of each of which appears to induce not only a different cognitive outcome (Milner 1967, Diamond and Goldman-Rakic 1986) but also a different affective outcome (Grafman et al. 1986). For present purposes, the term frontal lobe will be retained, pending further clarification of this structure's differential specialization.

Affective change following destruction of brain can be related to cognitive loss. But irritative lesions are apt to also generate epochs of disordered affect (negative or positive). They pose more complicated problems in interpretation than do static lesions. Sackeim et al. (1982), reviewing an extensive literature, concluded that seizure equivalents caricaturing positive affect more commonly originate in the left hemisphere and those caricaturing negative affect more commonly originate in the right. Their straightforward explanation was that each hemisphere thus exhibited its inherent affective propensity. Alternatively one could attribute the behavioral manifestation to an intrahemispheric imbalance. This hypothesis becomes somewhat attractive when one considers that each hemisphere in fact gave rise to either kind of affect in different instances, the dissociations between hemispheres being a matter of degree only. Not knowing the localization of the discharging foci, one cannot take this argument further with existing data.

Even the assumption that the discharging focus generates the behavior in question can be challenged. The intriguing personality changes that accompany temporal-lobe epilepsy are attributed by Bear and Fedio (1977) to excess interictal temporal-lobe activity ("temporal-limbic hyperconnection"). An alternative interpretation is that the temporal-lobe lesion results in disinhibition of parietal or limbic cortex and this in turn generates expressions of personal motives unqualified by an appreciation of the environmental contingencies.

It is instructive that physical brain damage in specific locations can simulate affective disorder, and it is an advance that this affective disorder is no longer, as in the past, routinely assumed to be secondary, the patient's reaction to his predicament. Nevertheless, when one considers such a finding, one should keep in mind the numerous alternative interpretations that remain viable.

NEUROPSYCHOLOGICAL FINDINGS IN DEPRESSION

When patients with psychopathology are given cognitive tests, they often show specific deficits even when cognitive deficiencies do not feature in the definition or even the description of the psychopathological entity. Psychopathic patients do poorly on frontal-lobe tests sensitive to impulsivity. Schizophrenics score poorly on certain left-hemisphere (verbal) measures. Depressed patients exhibit deficits in performances attributed to right-parietal lobe, largely of a visuospatial nature (Flor-Henry 1976; Goldstein et al. 1977; Kronfol et al. 1978; Taylor et al. 1979; Brumback et al. 1980; Wood et al. 1982; Flor-Henry et al. 1984). However, before inferring a focal cerebral deficit in such cases, one should review the nature of the test performance in light of the psychopathology to ensure that the results are not confounded by factors irrelevant to the focal brain deficit.

When speaking, schizophrenics are apt to drift off into task-irrelevant, thought-disordered verbalizations. They might score poorly on verbal tests for such nonspecific reasons. For their part, depressed people with psychomotor retardation would be expected to score poorly on timed tests. Many tests of visuospatial skills are timed. A concerted attempt to test regional cerebral hypotheses of schizophrenic and major affective disorder with neuropsychological procedures not subject to such confounding limitations appears not yet to have been undertaken. Discussion of the alleged right-parietal impairment of depressed individuals that follows is subject to the above reservation.

Laterality findings generally support the idea of right-sided hyperactivation in depression (Bruder and Yosawitz 1979; Wexler and Heninger 1979; Johnson and Crockett 1982). The expected right-ear advantage in a verbal analytic task is attenuated, but restored during remission (but see Moscovitch et al. 1981; also Chapter 4, this volume). Lateral gaze during reflective thinking is left biased, as would be expected if the right hemisphere is overactivated (Myslobodsky and Horesh 1978). Correspondingly, right-hemisphere electroconvulsive shock treatment is thought to be as effective as bilateral in facilitating remission in depression (Cohen et al. 1974).

The following neurological models could account for right-posterior cerebral insufficiency in depression: 1) that area of cortex is underactivated, 2) it is inhibited (transcallosally or by ipsilateral frontal cortex) or, 3) it is concurrently engaged in other (mentally disordered) activity that interferes with its test-related cognitive functions.

We learn something fundamental about brain organization from the neuropsychological test findings in psychopathology: that localization of cerebral function is not strictly modular. There must be enough superimposition of different activities upon a given area of brain, or enough scope for cross-talk interference within the neural network, for logically unrelated behavioral manifestations (such as negative affect and visuospatial processing) to influence each other.

In contrast to right-posterior cerebral insufficiency in depression, the right-frontal lobe gives indications of being overactivated (in terms of laterality as well as EEG findings, reviewed in Chapter 1). In that chapter Davidson suggests that the overactive right-frontal lobe inhibits the ipsilateral parietal lobe.

THE ACTIVITY CYCLE: A MODEL

We have noted that the interpretation of regional cerebral "dysfunction" in terms of disordered brain mechanisms is less straightforward than might appear. Given the many rival hypotheses that could be entertained, the best expedient at this time might be to search for parsimony; instead of blandly referring phenomena to otherwise unsubstantiated neurological "dysfunctions," an attempt should be made to explain as much as possible at the level of behavior. To do so one requires a model of how action and emotion interplay and of the cortical basis of their interaction (Kinsbourne and Bemporad 1984). I now present one such model, which I term the "activity cycle."

Pribram and McGuinness (1975) distinguish between two forms of cerebral alerting: arousal, which is a phasic response to a novel event, and activation, which is tonic preparedness for preprogrammed action. Following Tucker et al. (1978) I attribute a special role in arousal to the right hemisphere and in activation to the left hemisphere.

For reasons mentioned above, I have attributed to the left hemisphere a superordinate role in the biologically fundamental function of "approach" or the continuation of ongoing behavior. By virtue of left-hemisphere mechanisms the individual pursues his plan of the moment, monitoring its stepwise consequences by use of left-posterior cerebral input analyzers. As long as each successive act more closely approximates the anticipated state of affairs, ongoing behavior continues. While it continues, the individual feels motivated and, to the extent that a successful outcome is as yet uncertain, anxious (Tucker et al. 1978). When the plan is consummated, and a match has been achieved between the anticipated and the objectively attained state, ongoing activity is discontinued in the context of a subjective feeling of satisfaction.

Should a mismatch occur at any time during ongoing behavior between the anticipated and the actual state of affairs as monitored by left-posterior cortex, there results an orienting response to this novelty accompanied by an arrest of ongoing behavior. Subjectively the individual experiences a surge of negative emotion. In these manifestations of arousal the model assumes participation of the right hemisphere. In the usual course of events the individual is subsequently able to reprogram his activities to accommodate the unexpected event, so that ongoing behavior can be resumed. At such time the emotional surge is terminated, and the left hemisphere resumes its control of behavior. But if no ready solution is in sight, perhaps because the interfering event is beyond human control (e.g. a bereavement), then the emotional surge continues, as does the arrest of ongoing behavior, perhaps to the point of constituting a depressive reaction. The latter can then only be curtailed if the individual reconciles himself to the changed situation by changing his goals to new ones that are attainable. I suggest that the right-frontal lobe contributes the behavioral control and frustration tolerance required to implement such a change.

If a catastrophic event occurs, rendering futile any attempts to plan, the left-frontal lobe suspends its planning function. The right-frontal lobe becomes active in its efforts to control the emotional reaction when it has outlasted its adaptive value. This is an example of diminished activity of one cortical area being accompanied by increased activity of another, not through disinhibition at the neurological level, but because of a control shift within the organism adaptive to a changed circumstance. The right-posterior deficit in cognitive function could be explained as a spinoff of the control functions of the right-frontal lobe as already suggested, manifest electrophysiologically as a reciprocity in activation between right-anterior and right-posterior cortex (see Chapter 1). The inhibition of right-posterior function, in addition to controlling the emotional reaction, would be apt to impair this area's role in the detection of emotional cues and its sensitivity to pleasure-arousing stimuli. Anhedonia (Meehl 1962) would result. It is suggestive that anhedonics have been reported to exhibit impaired orienting response to novel stimuli (Miller 1986).

The cycle of events described above could characterize a normal mourning reaction. The victim of major affective disorder might enter into such a reaction after less environmental provocation than is normal and maintain it for a longer period of time (reflecting a vulnerability, the brain basis of which is unknown). Thus, in a recently completed study, we have found left frontal and right posterior neuropsychological test deficits in depressed children, but none on left posterior or right frontal tests.

The present model of affective reaction emphasizes the tight coordination of cognition and emotion and avoids any implication that emotions per se are represented in dedicated cerebral territories. (For a congruent viewpoint, see Wexler 1986.) Each affective state reflects a particular type of cognitively represented circumstance. In turn, cognitive reorganization is energized by the affective state. The cerebral cortex is implicated in affect by virtue of specific interactions with brain stem mechanisms (LeDoux 1986).

The respective roles of the hemispheres in activation and arousal are consistent with recent indications of neurochemical lateralization (see Chapter 2). An excess of dopamine projections is credited to the left hemisphere and that of norepinephrine to the right. Dopamine is involved in consummatory behavior (Snyder 1974), whereas norepinephrine mediates arousal in response to novelty (Tucker and Williamson 1984). Frontal connections predominate.

The above model provides a heuristic framework for further inquiry into the flow of events that sets up and sustains a depressive reaction. It is also applicable to the syndromes of hysteria (lack of frontal control of right-posterior cortex) and obsessive-compulsive disease (failure of the left hemisphere to acknowledge match based on comparison between schema and actuality). Even aspects of schizophrenia can be modeled as motivated behavior attended by anxiety but stripped of its relationship to the context of external circumstance. The model can also explain the regionally determined affective consequences of damage by stroke.

Left-frontal damage, as already indicated, disables planning, rendering events out of control and therefore calling excessively on the right-hemisphere compensatory mechanisms. Right-posterior damage blunts the individual's own arousal states, generating an anhedonia that fits under the rubric of depression but lacks the cognitive elaborations found with left-frontal-lobe disorder. Correspondingly, we predicted a qualitative difference in the type of depressive reaction elicited by left-frontal and right-posterior stroke (cognitive-anxious versus anhedonic-detached, respectively; see Kinsbourne and Bemporad 1984). Finset (1983) found support for this prediction in his data.

In the more severe primarily psychiatric depressive states, one would expect left-frontal and right-posterior deficits to coexist, because of the implication of both areas in the activity cycle. Left-posterior damage impairs the monitoring of the outside world, which would betray the presence of mismatch between intention and consequence of action. The patient remains in ignorance of his failures to proceed as planned, and this oblivious state translates into the indifference reaction observed by Starkstein and Robinson (see Chapter 2) and Finset (see Chapter 3). The patient with right-frontal disease lacks the control system that seeks to reconcile his personal goal with external reality. He therefore exhibits a different type of indifference reaction, notoriously antisocial and disinhibited (heedless of other people and external things).

Rapidly advancing technology is rendering it possible to test many predictions of the model through direct measurement of regional cerebral metabolism and electrical activity in a variety of psychopathological states. Although advances in this direction have been made (e.g., Kuhl et al. 1985; Guenther et al. 1986; Morihisa and McAnulty 1985), the most revealing findings would be expected to accrue from event-related measurements relating changes in regional cortical activity to changes in cognitive performance and mood.

CEREBRAL DYSFUNCTION IN DEPRESSION: TRAIT OR STATE MARKER?

The study of cerebral function in depression is largely motivated by the desire to discover a trait marker for major affective disorder. Such a marker could help predict the disease and identify at-risk family members. It might also clarify the contentious issue of childhood depression by indicating those sad, dysphoric, and maladaptively behaving children who are manifesting major affective disorder in a manner proper to their developmental level, to the exclusion of those whose psychiatric symptoms are otherwise to be accounted for. In contrast, a state marker would be specific to the depressed state but not to depressive illness. Negative affect, however caused, might be accompanied by its appearance, and as affect improves, the marker would become attenuated.

Based on the available evidence, cerebral dysfunction in depression can be parsimoniously explained as a state marker. Those studies that compare the patient in relapse and in remission find corresponding fluctuations in the value of the index of cerebral functioning that is being measured (Kronfol et al. 1978; Wexler and Heninger 1979; Brumback et al. 1980; Moscovitch et al. 1981; Tucker et al. 1981; Flor-Henry et al. 1984). More significantly still, it has proven possible to simulate aspects of depression-related cerebral dysfunction by inducing depressed mood in normal volunteers on a temporary basis (e.g., Ahern and Schwartz 1979; Tucker et al. 1981). It follows that patterns of cerebral dysfunction in depression are not specific to major affective disorder. Nor do they give any indication of what the cause of the major affective disorder might be.

If patterns of cerebral functioning in psychosis are state markers, then they will not prove to be diagnostic for particular nosological entities. Mental disease involves many and fluctuating affective reactions, and correspondingly variable cerebral involvement is to be expected. For example, depression, meeting *Diagnostic and Statistical Manual of Mental Disorders (Third Edition)* criteria for major affective disorder, occurs in up to 50 percent of schizophrenics (Johnson 1981). The depressive state will presumably add its related pattern of cerebral activity to whatever other cerebral activity pattern coexists with schizophrenia. The cerebral dysfunction that characterizes depression will prevail, whether the depressed individual is schizophrenic or not.

It is possible that state markers of cerebral dysfunction are superimposed on trait markers, as Sackeim and Decina (1983) suggested. But variations in peripheral and central laterality are well known to be nonspecific and are quite unpromising as markers specific to any one psychiatric entity.

Two Dimensions of Affect

The labels that are customarily used, positive emotions and negative emotions, imply a unitary dimension that lends itself to dichotomization and superimposition on the hemispheres. But following Tellegen (1985), Tucker (see Chapter 6) persuasively argues that there are two orthogonal dimensions: elation-depression and relaxation-anxiety. The former I consider associated with interruptive phenomena. A turn of events may engender either happiness or sadness, but in either case the emotion accompanies arrest of ongoing activity (because it succeeded—elation, or because it failed—depression). In contrast, calm and anxiety attend ongoing behavior. The individual may be confident of success or dubious of it. In either case, these feelings accompany the activity until it is completed.

Reasoning along the above lines, I align elation-depression with right-hemisphere activity and relaxation-anxiety with left-hemisphere activity.

If correct, this formulation has implications for the major currently contested issue in emotional lateralization: whether positive emotions relate to right- or left-hemisphere functioning. One would distinguish between the positive emotion of calm (during an activity) and joy (at its outcome). The former would be associated with left-hemisphere functioning, the latter with right hemisphere functioning. Whether this distinction clarifies findings hitherto considered in conflict remains to be determined.

The two types of depression proposed here conform to the above distinction. The left-anterior type relates to concern about inability to implement plans. It is characterized by anxiety. The right-posterior type is an anhedonia that leaves the patient unmoved by adversity as well as by normally pleasurable experiences; that is, a loss of emotional arousal across the board.

State Fluctuations and Variability in Laterality Findings

Any coherent integration of data on cerebral dysfunction must sacrifice completeness, in that conflicting findings have to be discarded (see Silberman and Weingartner 1986; also Chapter 4, this volume). The above discussion identifies trends in this literature, not easily replicable findings. There are numerous possible reasons why study outcomes might not agree, but one not usually mentioned is the variability that seems to inhere in much of psychopathology. If there were structural insufficiency or even well localized "dysfunction" in a particular hemispheric area, one would expect its hallmarks to be reliably elicted. The actual state of affairs is more consistent with the view that one is tapping fluctuating states of interacting cerebral mechanisms that are for unknown reasons unstable. Summarizing the dichotic-listening literature in psychopathology, Bruder (1983) noted that decreased lateralization for both verbal and nonverbal tasks is the rule in affective disorder. It does not follow, however, that the individual patient is structurally less lateralized in relapse than in remission. Fluctuation in control mechanisms that determine hemisphere usage can lead to different patients in a sample being tested in different states. Given that the normative null point for dichotic paradigms is biased (shifted to the right), even random fluctuations around this point must lead to a less asymmetric ("less lateralized") mean, there being less range available for excursion in the direction of more asymmetry than in the direction of less asymmetry. In bipolar disease, fluctuations appear to be particularly great, even leading to reversals in the direction of asymmetry (e.g., in half-field viewing; see Silberman et al. 1983). This does not prove that the language control area is actually shifting between hemispheres. Cerebral metabolic measurements vividly confirm variability of cerebral states in bipolars (see Chapter 5).

Concurrent activation is capable of reversing laterality findings (Kinsbourne and Byrd 1985; Kinsbourne and Bruce 1987), and the continual subvocalizations of schizophrenics are a potential source of concurrent activation.

Statistically significant group outcomes obscure the variability of the individual. Greater stability of measured parameters accompanies favorable treatment response (e.g., Ploog 1950; also Chapter 4, this volume). Serial measurements of parameters of interest on the same cases should disclose the instability of control mechanisms. This instability could characterize a given psychopathology (bipolar disease, attention deficit disorder) as much as does the flagrant bias of control mechanisms that generates its characteristic behavioral deviance.

I conclude that patterns of deviant cerebral activity that accompany mental disorders constitute the brain basis of the abnormal affect and cognition that characterizes each such disorder. Mental state and brain state are two sides of the same coin. No conclusion can be drawn from these mind-brain correspondences as to the causes of mental illnesses.

Reorganization of Cerebral Function in Depression

Wexler (Chapter 4) vividly illustrates the inadequacy of a quasi-structural approach to neuropsychological localization in psychopathology. If depression is characterized by local right-hemisphere "dysfunction" (e.g., Flor-Henry 1979; Gruzelier 1979), why do EEG, cerebral metabolism, and laterality findings all implicate other areas of cortex? If, instead, as I have argued, findings referable to cerebral cortex in depression indicate cerebral reorganization of cortical function in response to the affective disorder, deviations from normative functioning of diverse areas or cortex in both hemispheres would not be unexpected. There would be nothing anomalous about right-posterior impairment coexisting not only with right-anterior over-activation, but also with changed use of territories in the left hemisphere. As the activity cycle model shows, deviance in one phase of the cycle can affect any or all of the rest.

Suppose, for any reason, a person becomes anhedonic. Right-posterior activity is suspended. This deprives the individual of the basis for motivation to engage his left hemisphere. No plans are being made because the motivation to make them is lacking. Left-frontal underactivation results. In severe depression one would therefore expect both right-posterior and left-frontal neuropsychological abnormality.

It is possible, however, to envisage a disorder originating with left frontal underuse involving impulsive, ill-conceived behavior and instability in the face of uncontrolled contingencies, but without anhedonia or lack of motivation. Mild (neurotic or reactive) depression (Paykel et al. 1971) could be characterized in this way.

Interpretation of the Results of Special Tests

Laterality findings reflect the balance of activation between the hemispheres. Thus diminished right-ear advantage on a verbal test could indicate less activation of left hemisphere, more activation of right, or a combination of the two.

Changes in the electrical activity of the left hemisphere (discussed by Wexler in Chapter 4) do not show that hemisphere to be abnormal or impaired. They indicate that it is being differently used.

Changes in cerebral metabolism are even more difficult to interpret (for a sophisticated discussion, see Wood et al. 1982). Excitation and inhibition are both energy consuming, so no conclusion about the balance between these opponent processes can be based solely upon cerebral metabolic findings. Even that the level of metabolic activity reflects the level of usage of the territory in question is not totally clear. But if it does, changes in such use could be part of a reorganization of mental-neural processes in relation to the depressed affect. The territory in which such changes occur need not be deemed abnormal in the neurological sense. Neuropsychological measurements in depression should be viewed as documenting how cortical function reorganizes during depressed mental states (not what is "wrong" with the cortex in depression).

REFERENCES

Alema G, Rosadini G, Rossi GF: Psychic reactions associated with intracarotid amytal injection and relation to brain damage. Excerpta Medica. International Congress 37:154–155, 1961

Ahern GL, Schwartz GE: Differential lateralization for positive versus negative emotion. Neuropsychologia 17:693–697, 1979

Bear DM, Fedio P: Quantitative analysis of interictal behavior in temporal lobe epilepsy. Arch Neurol 34:454–467, 1977

Bick PA, Kinsbourne M: Auditory hallucinations and subvocal speech in schizophrenics. Am J Psychiatry 144:222–225, 1987

Blumer D, Benson DF: Personality changes with frontal and temporal lobe lesions, in Psychiatric Aspects of Neurologic Disease. Edited by Benson F, Blumer D. New York, Grune and Stratton, 1975

Borod JC, Koff E: Asymmetries in affective facial expression: behavior and anatomy, in the Psychobiology of Affective Development. Edited by Fox NA, Davidson RJ. Hillsdale, NJ, Erlbaum, 1984

Bruder GE: Cerebral laterality and psychopathology: a review of dichotic listening studies. Schizophr Bull 9:134–151, 1983

Bruder GE, Yozawitz A: Central auditory processing and lateralization in psychiatric patients, in Hemisphere Asymmetries of Function in Psychopathology. Edited by Gruzelier J, Flor-Henry P. Amsterdam, Elsevier, 1979

Brumback RA, Staton RD, Wilson H: Neuropsychological study of children during and after remission of endogenous depressive episodes. Percept Mot Skills 50:1163–1167, 1980

Cohen BD, Penick SB, Tarter RE: Antidepressant effects of unilateral electrical convulsive shock therapy. Arch Gen Psychiatry 31:673–675, 1974

Davidson RJ, Mednick D, Moss E, et al: Ratings of emotions are influenced by the visual field to which affective information is presented. Brain and Cognition 6:403–411, 1987

Diamond A, Goldman-Rakic PS: Comparative development of human infants and rhesus monkeys on cognitive functions that depend on prefrontal cortex. Neuroscience Abstracts 12:792, 1986

Drake RA, Bingham BR: Induced lateral orientation and persuasibility. Brain and Cognition 4:156–164, 1985

Finset A: Depressive behavior, outbursts of crying and emotional indifference in left hemiplegics. Paper presented at the Second International Symposium on Models and Techniques of Cognitive Rehabilitation. Indianapolis, IN, March 1982

Flor-Henry P: Lateralized temporal-limbic dysfunction in psychopathology. Ann NY Acad Sci 280:777–797, 1976

Flor-Henry P: On certain aspects of the localization of the cerebral systems regulating and determining emotion. Biol Psychiatry 14:677–698, 1979

Flor-Henry P, Yeudall LT: Neuropsychological investigation of schizophrenia and manic depressive psychoses, in Hemisphere Asymmetries of Function in Psychopathology. Edited by Gruzelier J, Flor-Henry P. Amsterdam, Elsevier, 1979

Flor-Henry P, Fromm D, Schopflocher D: Neuropsychological test performance in depressed patients before and after drug therapy. Biol Psychiatry 19:55–72, 1984

Fog E, Fog M: Cerebral inhibition examined by associated movements, in Minimal Cerebral Dysfunction. Edited by Bax M, MacKeith R. Clinics in Developmental Medicine, No. 10. Lavenham, Suffolk, Lavenham Press, 1963

Fox NA, Davidson RJ: Hemisphere substrates of affect: a developmental model, in the Psychobiology of Affective Development. Edited by Fox NA, Davidson RJ. Hillsdale, NJ, Erlbaum, 1984

Gage DF, Safer MA: Hemisphere differences in the mood state-dependent affect for recognition of emotional faces. J Exp Psychol 11:752–763, 1985

Gainotti G: Reactions "catastrophiques" et manifestations d'indifférence au cours des attentes cerebrales. Neuropsychologia 7:195–204, 1969

Goldberg E, Costa LD: Hemispheric differences in the acquisition and use of descriptive systems. Brain Lang 14:144–173, 1981

Goldstein SG, Filskov SB, Weaver LA, et al: Neuropsychological effects of electroconvulsive therapy. J Clin Psychol 33:798–806, 1977

Grafman J, Vance SC, Weingartner H, et al: The effect of lateralized frontal lesions on mood regulation. Brain 109:1127–1148, 1986

Grijalva LR: Emotional asymmetries reported by dichotically presented depressive and neutral somatic statements. Anchorage, University of Alaska, 1982 (M.S. dissertation)

Gruzelier J: Synthesis and critical review of the evidence for hemispheric asymmetries of function in psychopathology, in Hemisphere Asymmetries of Function in Psychopathology. Edited by Gruzelier J, Flor-Henry P. Amsterdam, Elsevier, 1979

Guenther W, Moser E, Mueller-Spahn F, et al: Pathological cerebral blood flow during motor function in schizophrenic and endogenously depressed patients. Biol Psychiatry 21:889–899, 1986

Gur RE: Left hemisphere dysfunction and left hemisphere overactivation in schizophrenia. J Abnorm Psychol 87:226–238, 1978

Hicks RE: Interhemispheric response competition between vocal and unimanual performance in normal adult human male. J Comp Psychol 89:50–60, 1975

Johnson DAW: Depression in schizophrenia: some observations on prevalence, etiology and treatment. Acta Psychiatr Scand [Suppl] 3:129–134, 1981

Johnson O, Crockett D: Changes in perceptual asymmetries with clinical improvement in depression and schizophrenia. J Abnorm Psychol 91:45–54, 1982

Kinsbourne M: The cerebral basis of lateral asymmetries in attention. Acta Psychologica 33:193–201, 1970

Kinsbourne M: Eye and head turning indicate cerebral lateralization. Science 176:539–541, 1972

Kinsbourne M: The control of attention by interactions between the cerebral hemispheres, in Attention and Performance IV. Edited by Kornblum S. New York, Academic Press, 1973

Kinsbourne M: Lateral interactions in the brain, in Hemispheric Disconnection and Cerebral Function. Edited by Kinsbourne M, Smith WL. Springfield, IL, Thomas, 1974

Kinsbourne M: The mechanisms of hemispheric control of the lateral gradient of attention, in Attention and Performance V. Edited by Rabbitt PMA, Dornic J. London, Academic Press, 1975

Kinsbourne M: Hemispheric specialization and the growth of human understanding. Am Psychol 37:411–420, 1982

Kinsbourne M, Bemporad B: Lateralization of emotion: a model and the evidence, in the Psychobiology of Affective Development. Edited by Fox NA, Davidson RJ. Hillsdale, NJ, Erlbaum, 1984

Kinsbourne M, Bruce R: Shift in visual laterality within blocks of trials. Acta Psychologica 66:139–156, 1987

Kinsbourne M, Byrd M: Word load and visual hemifield shape recognition: priming and interference effects, in Mechanisms of Attention: Attention and Performance XI. Edited by Posner MI, Marin OSM. Hillsdale, NJ, Erlbaum, 1985

Kinsbourne M, Cook J: Generalized and lateralized effects of concurrent verbalization of a unimanual skill. Q J Exp Psychol 23:341–345, 1971

Kinsbourne M, Hiscock M: Asymmetries of dual-task performance, in Cerebral Hemisphere Asymmetry: Methods, Theory and Application. Edited by Hellige J. New York, Praeger, 1983

Kolb B, Whishaw IO: Fundamentals of Human Neuropsychology. San Francisco, Freeman, 1980

Kronfol A, Hamsher K, Digre K, et al: Depression and hemispheric function: changes associated with unilateral ECT. Br J Psychiatry 132:560–567, 1978

Kuhl DE, Metter JE, Riege WH: Patterns of cerebral glucose utilization in depression, multiple infarct dementia and Alzheimer disease, in Brain Imaging and Brain Function. Edited by Sokoloff L. New York, Raven, 1985

LeDoux JE: The neurobiology of emotion, in Mind and Brain. Edited by LeDoux JE, Hirst W. Cambridge, Cambridge University Press, 1986

Lempert H, Kinsbourne M: Effects of laterality of orientation on verbal memory. Neuropsychologia 20:211–214, 1982

McGuigan FH: Covert oral behavior and auditory hallucinations. Psychophysiology 3:73–80, 1966

Meehl PE: Schizotaxia, schizotypy, schizophrenia. Am Psychol 17:827–838, 1962

Miller GA: Information processing deficits in anhedonia and perceptual aberration: a psychophysiological analysis. Biol Psychiatry 21:100–115, 1986

Milner B: Some effects of frontal lobectomy in man, in The Frontal Granular Cortex and Behavior. Edited by Warren J, Akert K. New York, McGraw-Hill, 1962

Milner B: See discussion in Rossi and Rosadini (1967)

Morihisa JM, McAnulty GB: Structure and function: images from brain electrical activity mapping and computed tomography in schizophrenia. Biol Psychiatry 20:3–19, 1985

Moscovitch M, Strauss E, Olds: Handedness and dichotic listening performance in patients with unipolar endogenous depression who received ECT. Am J Psychiatry 138:988–990, 1981

Myslobodsky MS, Horesh N: Bilateral electrodermal activity in depressive patients. Biol Psychiatry 6:111–120, 1978

Paykel ES, Prusoff B, Klerman GL: The endogenous-neurotic continuum in depression. J Psychiatr Res 8:73–90, 1971

Perris C, Monakhov K, Von Knorring L, et al: Systematic structural analysis of the EEG of depressed patients. Neuropsychobiology 4:207–228, 1978

Ploog D: "Psychische Gegenregulation" dargestellt am Verlaufe von Elektroschock Behandlungen. Archiv Psychiatrie Zeitschrift Neurologie 183:617–662, 1950

Poeck K: Pathophysiology of emotional disorders associated with brain damage, in Handbook of Clinical Neurology. Edited by Vinken PJ, Bruyn GW. Amsterdam, North-Holland, 1969

Posner M: Paper presented to the High Point Hospital Symposium on Attention Deficit Disorder. Laguna Beach, CA October 1986

Pribram KH, McGuinness D: Arousal, activation and effort in the control of attention. Psychol Rev 82:116–149, 1975

Robinson RG, Szetela B: Mood changes following left hemisphere brain injury. Ann Neurol 9:447–453, 1981

Rossi GF, Rosadini G: Experimental analysis of cerebral dominance in man, in Brain Mechanisms Underlying Speech and Language. Edited by Millikan CH, Darley FL. New York, Grune and Stratton, 1967

Sackheim HA, Decina P: Lateralized neuropsychological abnormalities in bipolar adults and in children of bipolar probands, in Laterality and Psychopathology. Edited by Flor-Henry P. New York, North-Holland, 1983

Sackheim HA, Greenberg MS, Weiman AL, et al: Hemispheric asymmetry in the expression of positive and negative emotions. Arch Neurol 39:210–218, 1982

Schneirla TC: An evolutionary and developmental theory of biphasic processes underlying approach and withdrawal, in Nebraska Symposium on Motivation. Edited by Jones MR. Lincoln, University of Nebraska Press, 1959

Schneirla TC: Behavioral development and comparative psychology. Q Rev Biol 41(no. 3), 1966

Schwartz GE, Davidson RJ, Maer F: Right hemisphere lateralization for emotion in the human brain: interactions with cognition. Science 19:286–288, 1975

Sherrington CS: The integrative action of the nervous system. New Haven, Yale University Press, 1906

Silberman EK, Weingartner H: Hemisphere lateralization of functions related to emotion. Brain and Cognition 5:322–353, 1986

Silberman EK, Weingartner H, Stillman R, et al: Altered lateralization of cognitive processes in depressed women. Am J Psychiatry 140:1340–1346, 1983

Snyder SH: Catecholamines as mediators of drug effects in schizophrenics, in The Neurosciences, Vol. 3. Edited by Schmitt FO, Worden EG. Cambridge, MIT Press, 1974

Taylor MA, Greenspan B, Abrams R: Lateralized neuropsychological dysfunction in affective disorder and schizophrenia. Am J Psychiatry 8:1031–1034, 1979

Tellegen A: Structures of mood and personality and their relevance to assessing anxiety, with an emphasis on self-report, in Anxiety and the Anxiety Disorders. Edited by Tuma AH, Maser JD. Hillsdale, NJ, Erlbaum, 1985

Terzian H: Behavioral and EEG effects of intracarotid sodium amytal injection. Acta Neurochirurgica 12:230–239, 1964

Tucker DM: Lateral brain function, emotion, and conceptualization. Psychol Bull 89:19–46, 1981

Tucker DM, Williamson PA: Asymmetric neural control systems in human self-regulation. Psychol Rev 91:185–215, 1984

Tucker DM, Antes JR, Stenslie CE, et al: Anxiety and lateral cerebral function. J Abnorm Psychol 87:380–383, 1978

Tucker DM, Stenslie CE, Roth RS: Right frontal lobe activation and right hemisphere performance. Arch Gen Psychiatry 38:169–174, 1981

Wexler BE: A model of brain function and its implications for psychiatric research: II. Br J Psychiatry 148:357–362, 1986

Wexler BE, Heninger GR: Alterations in cerebral laterality during acute psychotic illness. Arch Gen Psychiatry 36:278–284, 1979

Wood F, Ebert V, Kinsbourne M: The episodic-semantic memory distinction in memory and amnesia: clinical and experimental observations, in Human Memory and Amnesia. Edited by Cermak L. Hillsdale, NJ, Erlbaum, 1982

Wood F, Flowers L, Goode D, et al: Neurobehavioral memory deficits in schizophrenia versus bipolar disease: a neuropsychological and rCBF study. Paper presented to the International Congress for Schizophrenia Research. Miami, FL, March 1987

Yeudall LT, Fromm-Auch D: Neuropsychological impairments in various neuropathological populations, in Hemisphere Asymmetries of Function in Psychopathology. Edited by Gruzelier J, Flor-Henry P. Amsterdam, Elsevier, 1979

Chapter 8

Conceptual and Methodological Issues in Neuropsychological Studies of Depression

David Galin, M.D.

Chapter 8

Conceptual and Methodological Issues in Neuropsychological Studies of Depression

This volume is an extraordinarily stimulating collection! I am enthusiastic because this varied set of papers, taken together, indicates that we are beginning to ask the right questions, powerful questions, that put us within reach of a comprehensive neuropsychological understanding of depression. Such a synthesis has not yet arrived, but the ideas sketched in this symposium give some idea of the shape it will take when it comes. This will be heartening to those among us, both new students and jaded specialists, who have been confused and discouraged by the shifting nosology, the proliferation of high-tech methods they cannot understand or afford, and the apparent need to choose the "chemical" way or the "psychodynamic" way or the "information-processing" way.

My assignment is to provide an overview for this volume and some constructive commentary. First I will offer some personal opinions on research strategy that I believe apply to all research on the relationships between brain and behavior. Then I will examine some pervasive problems of definition concerning our concepts of emotion, localization of function, and lateral specialization. Finally, rather than address each chapter, I will discuss just a few that I believe are illustrative of the issues raised by the rest. I will underline what seem to me to be the solid contributions and also the points of method and interpretation about which reasonable persons might disagree. My intention is to assist the reader in relating these particular chapters to the field as a whole.

The general question that this symposium addresses is: what can we say about the brain mechanisms related to depression? Let me amplify this question to highlight what we need to accomplish. Depression is a phenomenon at the psychological level of analysis, and we want to account for it in terms of some units of brain function. But the units are different at different levels of analysis: at the chemical level we have such units as norepinephrine and dopamine; at the physiological level we have electroencephalogram (EEG) alpha amplitudes and coherences; at the anatomical level we have hemispheres, or lobes, or cytoarchitectonic fields; at the information-processing level we have appraisals and reactions and communications. There is not a one-to-one correspondence between the units at one level and the units at the next. Is there one level of analysis that is *really* the best for accounting for depression (effects at other levels being secondary), or do we need a multilevel account?

Overall, this volume favors theory, with three totally theoretical papers and much theory in several others. While I am not advocating theory instead of data, I am grateful that we have avoided still another catalogue of empirical observations collected without a theoretical context. Too often researchers seem to say, "We have this expensive machine which measures variable X, so let's measure variable X in this population too," and they produce what we could call opportunistic correlational studies. A good new theory will lead us to collect the right data, not just more data. The data that we already have and do not understand are drawn from several levels of analysis (e.g., chemical, neurological, psychological, social), and we need an integrative theory.

This collection's emphasis on theory will also be useful to residents and other students who are trying to develop a conceptual framework on which to arrange all the clinical anecdotes, experimental reports, and current orthogonal theories. In addition, the quality of the experimental work reported is very high, and the papers provide good reviews, or at least points of entry, into the widely scattered literature. They cover a range of different methods, populations, and levels of analysis: ablations and natural lesions, electrophysiology, infants and animals, neurochemistry, position emission tomography (PET), computed tomography (CT), regional cerebral blood flow, hemifield and dichotic stimulation, dual task interference studies. It must be noted that some important areas are not mentioned: electroconvulsive treatment, psychopharmacology, and endocrine-central nervous system relations.

I recommend, particularly for the nonspecialist, an attitude of constructive skepticism toward reviews of the literature in a field in which there is still so much less than perfect consensus. Some reviews may be selective, citing only those that support the author's view. Others strive for completeness, and in their passion to remain unbiased, they give papers that have 5 subjects in a group as much space as they give those with 50 in each group. Often, these reviews conclude with a simple majority vote: "the weight of evidence indicates. . . ." I am against democracy in this instance: several inadequate studies cannot be combined to add up to a valid conclusion. This includes studies that are inadequate not because their authors were incompetent, but simply because at the time the studies were done the variables that we *now* recognize as critical had not been identified. If we would consider a study done now as hopelessly confounded if it did not control for X or Y, then we should not cite as evidence earlier data that could not have controlled for X and Y.

SOPHISTICATION OF THE NEW MODELS

Neuropsychological models have become increasingly sophisticated compared to those of just 10 years ago. This is reflected in the chapters in this volume, particularly in two areas: affect and lateral specialization.

New Role for Affect

I am choosing the term "affect" to designate the entire area of mental, behavioral, and physiological phenomena with which we are concerned. As the concept of affect has become more differentiated (discussed below, under "Definitions and Distinctions in the Domain of Affect"), neuropsychologists, and even cognitive psychologists (Bower 1981, 1983; Mandler 1984), are giving it more of a role in the *organization* of the mind. This is exemplified in Chapters 1, 4, 6, and 7.

Affect was once viewed as sharply distinct from cognition and relatively primitive, depending only on "lower" parts of the brain. It was elicited automatically like a reflex; the physiological components were seen as facilitating elemental action processes like the four F's, and the subjective components were considered epiphenomenal like the rest of consciousness.

The newer perspective recognizes that affect is a global, or emergent, property of a functioning complex system, and it cannot be dissected out of the brain (or out of behavior) and studied in isolation any more than one could take apart a car and examine the parts of it that are "transportation." Therefore, the emphasis has shifted toward better specification of the components of the system and the functional relationships among them. The distinction between affect and cognition is no longer so clear. In his neuropsychological model of an "activity cycle," Kinsbourne, (Chapter 7) has illustrated the importance of considering the whole person acting adaptively within the context of a complex environment. Wexler has gone further and proposed that affect *is* the framework or organizer for cognition and action; I particularly want to recommend his recent paper in which this idea is more fully developed (Wexler 1986). Tucker (Chapter 6) emphasizes the relation of affective state to arousal and attention controls. He examines two perspectives: 1) a top-down model in which cognitive appraisal determines mood and in which the different cognitive organization of the left and right hemispheres leads to differential roles in affect; and 2) a bottom-up model, related to Wexler's, in which different affects exert specific influences on attention and cognition.

Transcending Naive Localicationism and Dichotomania

The notion that there is a relation between the duality of the human brain and other dualities in human nature has been taken up widely, even outside of neuropsychology. Like many productive ideas, this one is sometimes applied overenthusiastically. The specialization of the two halves of the brain has been offered as the mechanism underlying everybody's favorite pair of polar opposites: scientist-artist, obsessive-hysteric, rational-mystical, conscious-unconscious, masculine-feminine. Marcel Kinsbourne coined the term "Dichotomania" for this phenomenon in its excesses (Galin 1976).

This problem is a new version of "naive localizationism," the tendency to assign complex mental functions to "centers" in local regions of the brain, in the manner of the phrenologists.

The dichotomania of the 1970s, which focused on the differences between the hemispheres, is being replaced by concern with how the two hemispheres interact: they can be inhibitory, facilitatory, complementary, or independent (see for example Sprague 1966, in which a second lesion restores sight to a blind half-field; Bogen and Bogen 1969; Zaidel 1983; Hellige 1983; Galin 1974; Galin 1977; Galin et al. 1979). The emphasis on differences grew naturally out of excitement over the split-brain studies, in which direct interaction between hemispheres had been eliminated, but when the same paradigms (e.g., hemifield stimulation) were applied to normal subjects they were often interpreted without taking into account the role of the intact commissures. In this volume, interactions are usually explicitly considered.

The present phase is dominated by *intra*hemispheric distinctions, particularly between front and back. All of the contributors to this volume have stressed the differences between anterior and posterior regions. In fact, the interest generated by the important findings concerning front/back distinctions can be expected to lead to another dichotomanic phase featuring this dimension. However, we have made progress; it was the interactions and not just the differences between these regions that were particularly emphasized by Davidson, Kinsbourne, Wexler, and Tucker. Just what these interactions are remains rather vague, but I agree with these authors that there is a pony in there somewhere.

I had hoped for more attention to the up/down dimension, but it was barely represented at all. This is remarkable since affect has for so long been associated with subcortical structures. Cortical chauvinism is still very powerful. However, I am sure the balance will soon be corrected because of the increased availability of technologies for studying subcortical structures: CT, PET, regional cerebral blood flow, and magnetic resonance imaging (MRI). The prospects for MRI are particularly exciting; it will soon be as widely available as CT is now, and since it does not entail radiation or invasive procedures, it can be used in studies of normal subjects and children and even in longitudinal studies. In vivo MRI spectroscopy is rapidly developing, and soon MRI will be able to provide specific metabolic maps (now only available with PET) in addition to the high-resolution anatomical data it already provides.

In the present volume, there is almost no mention of the temporal lobe. One usually expects to see a lot about the medial temporal structures like the uncus and amygdala in a book about brain mechanisms and affect. Perhaps the omission has to do in part with the focus on anterior versus posterior, or action versus perception. The temporal lobe seems to have been assigned to the "posterior," but it really could be assigned a one-dimensional functional axis of its own, running from posterior-lateral to anterior-medial.

The dangers of naive localizationism notwithstanding, the very solid observations on regional differences reported here underscore the need for more intrahemispheric differentiation. It seems to me that we could happily give up thinking in terms of "lobes." We already know enough about each "lobe" to distinguish several subsystems within it; to the extent that the spatial resolution of our experimental techniques permits, we should use the subsystems as our anatomical unit of analysis. We already know that the medial frontal cortex has a very different role in the organization of action than the dorsolateral cortex (Goldberg 1985), and that orbital-basal regions are particularly involved with visceral responses. The differences between regions within each frontal lobe are much more striking than the differences between the left and the right (Milner and Petrides 1984). Roland puts it even more strongly: in concluding a summary of the functional specificity of small regions of the frontal lobe demonstrated in PET and blood flow studies, he says, "It is absurd now to speak about *the* function of the prefrontal cortex" (Roland 1984). Of course, we are limited somewhat by our methods: stroke lesions follow the distribution of the vessels, not the cytoarchitectonic boundaries; scalp recordings cannot get at medial and basal regions; and in animal experiments where these limits can be overcome, we do not know the analogs for depression, inappropriate cheerfulness, or shame. Nevertheless, if we do not limit our thinking to "lobes," we are more likely to find solutions to these problems.

However, we should not expect a one-to-one correspondence between regional brain subsystems, however finely differentiated, and the symptoms of depression (such as "anergy/initative = supplementary motor cortex"), because it is almost certain that the psychological units of analysis depend on the integration of several functional subsystems that are widely distributed anatomically.

DEFINITIONS AND DISTINCTIONS IN THE DOMAIN OF AFFECT

The words "emotion," "affect," "feeling," and "mood" are used differently by different writers, and sometimes they are used synonymously. Sometimes they refer particularly to a subjective component, and sometimes to much more. Until there is general agreement on usage, it is essential that we be explicit about our own definitions.

Several theories have pointed out important differences among emotion, mood, and affective style (Tomkins 1980; Ekman 1984; Izard 1977; Davidson 1984). For example, Ekman would distinguish different manifestations along one particular dimension of affect as follows: a brief reaction of "sadness" to a photo of a dead loved one would be called an *emotion*, a "blue" feeling that was present without apparent cause upon awakening in the morning and that persisted for hours would be called a *mood*; a character like Eeyore in Winnie-the-Pooh whom we call "melancholy" would be said to have an *affective style or trait*. Similarly, Ekman would distinguish anger (emotion), irritability (mood), and hostility (trait). These are not just differences in intensity or duration.

For Davidson and Ekman, an emotion is a complex reaction to a specific stimulus, usually lasting only seconds. The reaction is complex in that it involves a patterned response from several different systems: usually but not always it includes a subjective response, a distinctive facial expression, vocal responses, and changes in skeletal, autonomic, and endocrine activity. At least some of these patterned multimodal responses are relatively specific for particular emotions, (e.g., anger, fear, sadness, disgust, surprise). While some patterns are learned, at least some can be elicited by specific stimuli from all people, regardless of culture, probably "hard-wired" during phylogenetic history.

According to Ekman (1984), a mood is distinguished from an emotion in part by its long duration, persisting for hours or days. Whereas emotion is a brief, phasic response to a specific elicitor, mood is a tonic process. During the mood the corresponding emotion may be more easily elicited, persist longer, or be more intense than usual. Mood can be thought of as a condition in which the threshold for the related emotion has changed, but it is not simply a prolonged emotional reaction. A mood is characterized by a subjective state, but in between discrete emotional responses it has no distinctive facial display or pattern of autonomic activity. Not much is known about its elicitors or biological underpinnings. It is not clear that there is a specific eliciting stimulus for a mood, or what particular coping responses may terminate it.

Affective style or trait refers to some aspect of personality or character that is longer lasting than a mood, perhaps lifelong. It is a tendency to respond with a particular emotional reaction or to be prone to a particular mood.

Given these definitions, we can define an affective disorder as a condition in which the intensity, duration, or situational appropriateness of emotion or mood are maladaptive and interfere with work, relationships, and vegetative functioning. "Impulse disorder" and the "catastrophic reaction" seem to refer to abnormal emotional reactions; "flat affect" seems to refer to an abnormal absence of emotional reactions; and "inappropriate cheerfulness" and "depression" seem (most often) to refer to a mood.

It is clear that many of the observations reported in this volume concern different manifestations of affect, sometimes mood, sometimes one or another aspect of the emotional response complex. It will help us a great deal in resolving apparent conflicts if we are precise about just which phenomena we are talking about. Davidson in his studies of frontal EEG activity is usually dealing with emotional reactions, not moods, and he identifies them by the movement of certain facial muscles. Finset limits his definition of depressed mood to the subjective state and persistent facial and postural expression of sadness and explicitly leaves out thought content and vegetative components. For Starkstein and Robinson, depressed mood is defined by the summary scores of the Zung, Hamilton, and Present State Examination scales. On these scales a patient without Finset's defining symptoms could be rated as depressed on the basis of anhedonia and some selection of anergy, vegetative complaints, anxiety, and guilt. Neither reactions of sadness nor "blue" moods are sufficient or even necessary conditions for the diagnosis of depression, according to the *Diagnostic and Statistical Manual of Mental Disorders (Third Edition) (DSM-III)*.

In the above discussion, emotional reactions were presented phenomenologically, rather isolated from any perceptual, cognitive, or adaptive context. Theorists such as Tomkins, Ekman, Izard, and Davidson consider emotional reactions as part of a control system that regulates interactions with the environment. I will briefly outline such an account of affective behavior that Ekman proposed heuristically (1977), which is useful because it provides explicit names for subprocesses not usually distinguished by neuropsychologists.

Ekman uses Tomkins' term "affect program" to refer to the entire mechanism that stores, executes, and coordinates the patterns for each emotion's complex of responses (e.g., facial, vocal, autonomic, and subjective). The affect program is presumably distributed over several neural structures.

"Elicitors" are classes of stimuli or events that are appraised quickly, perhaps automatically, as the occasion for one or another emotion. All stimuli of each class have the same sort of personal relevance. They may be learned or "hard-wired." Presumably an elicitor could be an internal as well as an external event.

The "appraisal system" determines when the affect program becomes operative. It recognizes elicitors and activates the appropriate part of the affect program. Ekman proposes that the automatic appraisal system is differentiated from other cognitive evaluation systems that might be slower, sometimes conscious, that might provide more extensive characterization of stimuli, and that might eventually trigger the affect program.

"Coping" refers to controlled and automatic processes that modulate the components of the affect program: augmenting, reducing, or sustaining what is occurring. It may act internally (e.g., damping the autonomic response or inhibiting the facial expression or the subjective experience), or externally (e.g., fleeing or attacking). Coping includes cognitive activity. According to Davidson, coping can be thought of as directed toward managing the activated affect program rather than managing the elicitor per se.

This schema seems to me very useful for organizing our thoughts about brain mechanisms related to affective disorder. It is clear that there could be a breakdown in the phase of appraisal, in the affect program, or in the phase of coping. The appraisal of the nature and degree of relevance of a stimulus could be biased with respect to one or more emotions and could be hyper- or hyposensitive. The threshold for release of the affect program could be too high or too low, or certain components of the program could be absent or hyperactive (e.g., the subjective response, the facial display, or the autonomic response). The coping mechanisms might be slow, inaccurate, or overreactive. Our neuropsychological understanding of depression will advance faster if we are more precise about just what components of affect are disordered.

We *are* making progress in being more specific. Sinyor et al. (1986) used the Zung scale but explicitly assessed vegetative symptoms separately from mood and thought content. Davidson (Chapter 1), in interpreting his frontal EEG activation findings, invokes alternative explanations based on the appraisal process or the coping process. The excellent paper by Ross and Rush (1981) on the problems of diagnosis of depression in brain-damaged patients offers case histories that demonstrate the utility of more precise differentiation. Ross and Rush emphasize the need to distinguish among the nonverbal displays of emotion (facial expression, postures, prosody), particularly in patients with right-hemisphere lesions, and to distinguish what is communicated by these behaviors from the verbal reports of mood and ideas. They stress the necessity of obtaining a history and current account from family members, as well as from the patient. Finset (Chapter 3) also distinguishes among the affective changes following right-hemisphere lesions: indifference, denial, lack of initiative, "shallowness" of response, and mood versus thought content versus vegetative symptoms.

Finset has provided another great service by pointing out that "catastrophic reaction" is not synonymous with depression: "The immediate manifestation of the catastrophic reaction is, according to Goldstein, anxiety; depression occurs more as its prolonged aftereffect" (Chapter 3). He clarifies just what was demonstrated in the important paper by Gainotti (1972), which is so often miscited as showing that depression is more common following left lesions than right. In fact, Gainotti assessed specific behaviors indicating "depressive orientation of mood," separating them from the behaviors by which he defined the catastrophic reaction (primarily anxious and irritable, but including bursts of tears). Vegetative symptoms were not assessed. He found that depressed mood by this definition was *not significantly different* in the two groups. Only the catastrophic reaction was more frequent following left lesions. The miscitations may have arisen because in the summary of the paper Gainotti omits the finding of no left-right difference on the depressed mood variables and uses the hyphenated term "depressive-catastrophic" reaction.

Gainotti went further and distinguished between the incidence of specific affective behaviors in patients with different types of aphasia. He found that their catastrophic reactions were qualitatively different. Bursts of tears occurred in 68 percent of the 19 Broca's patients and in 0 percent of the 16 Wernicke's patients. I urge the reader to resist translating Broca's as equivalent to anterior and Wernicke's as posterior; we have no evidence as to the location, size, or age of the lesions. But Gainotti's data show the potential utility of being more precise about which components of affect are disordered.

The above distinctions are based on clinical or theoretical grounds. An empirical, data-driven approach is exemplified by the factor analysis of the Hamilton scale by Rhoades and Overall (1983). With oblique axis rotation, they find seven relatively independent factors that they label as somatization, reality disturbance, diurnal variation, sleep disturbance, mood depression, weight loss, and anxiety/agitation. Scores on these factors were used to empirically classify a large sample of patients and resulted in five groupings with distinctive factor-score profiles: suicidal, somaticizing, anxious, vegetative, and paranoid depressive. It cannot be emphasized too strongly that the factors that can be found are always constrained by the list of variables that go into the analysis: this set of profiles is what could be made from the Hamilton variables. Of course, the subcategories derived by such data-driven methods need external validation as much as the clinically derived subcategories. Nevertheless, this is another important approach.

There are a few other points of terminology about which I have some concern. The notion that the right hemisphere is specialized for affective processes was fairly rapidly retrenched to "just some" affective processes. But which ones? It was suggested that the right hemisphere dominated for negative affect and the left hemisphere for positive; the dichotomizing urge continues to assert itself. But "negative" and "positive" have never been clearly defined. The terms usually are used synonymously with "pleasant" and "unpleasant." Let us consider the seven emotions that Ekman considers basic because they are characterized by a universally recognized facial expression, independent of culture: happiness, sadness, anger, fear, disgust, surprise, and contempt. There is some ambiguity about sadness and fear; some people cultivate such experiences (e.g., "tear-jerker" movies, roller coasters). Happiness is the only one that is unambiguously "positive"; surprise might be pleasant or not. Ekman and Friesen (1975) have suggested that it would be useful to distinguish several sorts of "happy" and have proposed five types for consideration: sensory pleasure, amusement, relief of intense arousal, enhancement of self-esteem, and a state associated with novelty, excitement, or challenge. Until we get clear definitions for "positive" and "negative," we will be much better off referring to the specific emotions intended.

Now that we have considered some of the problems of definition and conceptual distinctions, let us turn to the specific contents of some of the chapters in this volume.

STARKSTEIN AND ROBINSON: MOOD DISORDERS FOLLOWING STROKE

Dr. Robinson and his colleagues have contributed two new major pieces of information to the neuropsychology of affect. First, depression is much more common following acute left-anterior strokes than strokes elsewhere, and it seems to be a direct result of the lesion rather than a secondary reaction to associated sensory, motor, or cognitive disability. Second, in the rat, right-hemisphere lesions produce hyperactivity and marked bilateral decreases in norepinephrine and dopamine, while left-hemisphere lesions have no effect. Both of these findings are very surprising; they are not accounted for by any current theory of depression or brain organization. They place major constraints on any new models of depression and open up many new opportunities for research.

Before discussing the content, I want to detail my appreciation for Robinson's style and methods, particularly for the benefit of whatever beginning students may be reading this. I have recently been teaching an introductory course in "Research Methods in Brain-Behavior Relations," and have used Dr. Robinson's research program, and particularly his 1984 paper in *Brain,* as an example of how-it-should-be-done. The research is focused, yet very broadly based and multidisciplinary, requiring sophistication at the chemical, anatomical, and psychological levels of analysis. I greatly admire the scope and the thoroughness of the research and in addition the manner of the published reports themselves.

Robinson's data papers are exemplary in their completeness, presenting enough of the methodological details so that the results can be evaluated and presenting enough of the data so that the conclusions can be evaluated. Because of space limitations, Starkstein and Robinson's chapter in this volume could only present an overview. Relatively large samples have been used, and the observations have been repeated on successive samples. The description of patients is fuller than usual (e.g., associated sensory and motor deficits, age, social history, time since injury, prior strokes, prestroke personality, and family history of depression). Robinson actually tested the reliability and validity of the measures he was using to assess depression and disability (Robinson et al. 1983; Starr et al. 1983). Although many of them were "standardized" tests, he was concerned about their reliability *in his population*. This is not common enough in our field. When there is a problem with the reliability or validity of a measure (such as with the CT evaluation of the borders of a fresh infarct), he states it plainly (Robinson et al. 1985, p. 225).

In several ways Robinson has followed up early observations with more and more rigorous control of the variables of interest. For example, the early results on relatively unselected patients were followed up with analyses on the subset who had CT evidence of only a single unilateral lesion and also by examining the effects of the presence and order of bilateral lesions on the mood disorder. The natural strokes in humans were followed up in animal studies first with artificial stroke (middle cerebral artery ligation) and subsequently with discrete suction lesions restricted to cortex. Robinson has begun to examine his patients longitudinally in order to evaluate the time course and stability of their symptoms and their response to treatment. He has distinguished between differences in the incidence and in the severity of mood disorder.

Dr. Robinson is very balanced in the claims he makes for his findings. In spite of the dramatic practical and theoretical implications of his results, he states his conclusions modestly and carefully; he warns against overgeneralizing his findings too far beyond the populations and the circumstances of the observations; he presents his results as an opening for further research rather than as *the* answer.

Of course, there are many others besides Robinson who possess these virtues, and I do not mean to slight any of our colleagues by using him as the exemplar. I am simply grateful to be able to illustrate for the students the possibility of programmatic, systematic research; clear, thorough reporting; and responsible interpretation of results, and to underline, by contrast, what is missing in much of the literature.

However, this is still an imperfect world, and there are a number of points at which I must take issue with Robinson and his colleagues.

Depression Associated with Left-Anterior Stroke

Starkstein and Robinson make two points: first, that depression is most associated with left-anterior lesions; and second (a much stronger position), the closer the lesion to the frontal pole, the higher the incidence and severity of the depression. The data certainly support the first position, but I have reservations about the second, for the following reasons.

The quality of the lesion localization depends on CT scan data, taken at variable times poststroke, when the lesion was still evolving histologically. As edema resolves, phagocytosis removes infarcted tissue, and glial scarring develops, the CT image of the lesion may temporarily disappear entirely, as factors making for lucency are balanced by factors causing opacity. In fact, in the longitudinal study, "in one third of patients the lesion did not visualize" (Robinson et al. 1985, p. 225). This raises concern about how accurately the lesions could be localized in at least some of the remaining two-thirds. The concern is not entirely relieved by the consideration that similar results were found in the chronic stroke population in which the CT scans were done months after the infarct (Robinson and Szetela 1981).

Let us assume that the CT data represent the actual borders of the infarcts well enough. It might still be argued that the correlation of depression with distance from the frontal pole is an artifact of the size of the lesion; infarcts that are bigger will be more likely to extend closer to the frontal pole, but also are more likely to involve other structures. Robinson did, in fact, examine the effect of lesion size, using a total volume measure; volume *was* correlated with depression ($r = 0.72$) in the anterior group, but not in the posterior group or in both groups combined, and was not related to mood changes in the right-hemisphere group (Robinson et al. 1984a).

In addition to volume, the shape of the lesion must be taken into account. A long, thin lesion extending more anteriorly could have the same volume as a more spherical lesion. What counts is which structures are destroyed or disconnected.

I would be happier with an analysis of lesion location in relation to the substructures of the anterior regions, as discussed above under the heading of "Transcending Naive Localizationism and Dichotomania." To begin with, was the lesion superficial or deep? How much did it involve the caudate or connections to it? Did it involve the insula or other temporal lobe structures, or connections to them? To what extent did the lesion impinge on or *disconnect* the orbital-basal, the dorsolateral, and the medial dorsal cortex? It appears that the supplementary motor area plays an important role in "internally" initiated action, while dorsolateral premotor cortex is most involved in organizing movements in reaction to an external stimulus (Goldberg 1985). Therefore, involvement of the supplementary motor area might be expected to be associated with the symptoms of anergy and lack of initiative. These symptoms could also be produced by lesions in other parts of the behavioral subsystem to which they contribute, but we would certainly expect to see them if the lesion seriously compromised the supplementary motor area.

Furthermore, the correlation of depression with distance from the pole for the anterior group was reduced by including the posterior group. This is contrary to what would be predicted from Robinson's hypothesis that the "graded" effect depends on disruption of noradrenergic cortical fibers that fan out progressively as they project from anterior to posterior. It could be explained by either the inherent instability of the correlations with small samples, or by postulating that the left-posterior depressions are due to other factors.

The plot shown by Robinson et al. (1984a) could be interpreted as showing a bimodal distribution, rather than a continuous "graded" effect. Demonstrating a continuous effect may require a larger sample, and it may require covering a larger range of each variable. The authors point out that the lesions did not cover the entire hemisphere, only the middle two-thirds, and there was some overlap in the territories covered by the anterior and posterior groups; "anterior" lesions were only "relatively" more anterior. Although the samples started out with over 100 cases, they shrank as patients were dropped for multiple lesions, poor CT, or previous history. The total remaining sample was then divided into left and right, and again into anterior and posterior. The sample size for each cell in the analysis got smaller, and the correlations got increasingly unstable. Changes of one or two patients can then make a big difference.

In addition to the claim for the left hemisphere, Robinson also believes that the mood disorder with right-hemisphere lesions and the hyperactivity and neurotransmitter changes in the rats are a graded function of distance of the lesion from the frontal pole. I am not yet convinced by the evidence for this claim in these contexts either, but I would like to stress that each of these data sets could be treated as independent of the others; there *may* be a graded effect in one hemisphere and not the other, or in the norepinephrine depletion in rats but not the mood in humans, and so forth.

With respect to the correlation of right-hemisphere lesion location and mood disorder (reversed from the left; the further from the frontal pole the greater the depression), all of the above comments apply. In addition, Robinson has his own caveats. Since the level of depression was less than that for left-hemisphere lesions, the range of scores was lower, and the correlation reported was "heavily dependent on two patients with posterior lesions and moderate to severe depression" (1984b). At the 6-month follow-up this correlation *reversed*, with the development of severe depression in two patients with anterior lesions, one of whom had previously been in the "inappropriately cheerful" group (1984a). The correlation became significant in the other direction even though the sample size had decreased due to attrition before follow-up.

The results of Sinyor et al. (1986) add to the puzzle. In their attempted replication of the results of Robinson et al. (1984b), they had a sample of the same size, and they controlled for all the factors that Robinson indicated (present volume) as critical. They also concluded that lesion location affects poststroke depression, but their results differed from those of Robinson and colleagues. They found no significant difference between left- and right-lesion groups in severity of depression, even considering anterior and posterior groups separately. In the left-hemisphere patients they found only a non-significant trend for greater depression with lesions closer to the frontal pole. In the *right-hemisphere* patients they found a strong *nonlinear* correlation: more depression with lesions both closest to and farthest from the frontal pole.

Robinson has suggested that the depression seen in the immediate poststroke period may be the direct result of the lesion and that the depression developing later may be indirect, i.e., "reactive" to the patients' disability. It may take a while for the patients to recognize the extent of their loss of capacity and the disruption of their lives. The patients studied by Sinyor et al. were not as acute as those studied by Robinson et al.; approximately 8 weeks versus 10 days poststroke. The patients studied by Sinyor et al. were in a rehabilitation hospital; perhaps that sample contained more of the reactive patients. However, the difference in time since stroke by itself is not a completely convincing explanation of the discrepancy, since Robinson found the same results in his earlier studies of chronic stroke patients that he did in his studies of acute patients. There were other sample differences that might contribute: Robinson's sample had a large proportion of black, lower-class men; Sinyor's sample population was half female and Jewish. Larger samples, better characterization of the lesions, and attention to the evolution of the symptoms over time will resolve these questions.

Behavioral and Neurochemical Changes Following Cerebral Lesions in Rats

The demonstration in rats of marked, bilateral, neurochemical changes following *right* but not left cortical lesions is very important. This finding could revolutionize our models of brain organization. Robinson followed up his initial studies, which used middle cerebral artery ligations, with a study using small suction lesions restricted to cortex, with both anterior and posterior locations (Robinson 1979; Pearlson et al. 1984).

As in the human stroke studies, Robinson and his colleagues interpret the results of this experiment as showing a "graded" effect proportional to the distance of the lesion from the frontal pole. I have reservations about this interpretation in this study, too. The lesions were placed at four locations, but not evenly spaced from anterior to posterior; two were anterior and close together (centers at 9.65 mm and 8.62 mm anterior to the earbars), the next was at 3.99 mm, and the next at 1.4 mm. The two anterior sites produced approximately the same depletion of norepinephrine, and the more caudal of the two produced a greater depletion of dopamine in the caudate. The next most caudal lesion had no effect on cortical norepinephrine, but had as great an effect on ipsilateral locus coeruleus norepinephrine and a greater effect on caudate dopamine than the most anterior lesion (Pearlson et al. 1984, Table 1). These data clearly show the importance of inter- and intrahemisphere location, but do not seem to be best described as representing a graded anterior-posterior effect.

It is attractive to put the animal work and the human stroke work together into a single story, but I am concerned that it is premature. I do not know how to go from the strictly unilateral right-lesion effects in the rat to the left-anterior-lesion effects in the human, or from the hyperactivity in the rat to the depressive symptoms in the human. It is also difficult to relate the rat's hyperactivity to the depletion of norepinephrine. The story is still incomplete.

Neuroendocrinology is developing into an important new dimension to be considered in the study of higher mental processes. The dexamethasone suppression test in depression is just one example. Recent research shows many functional relationships between cortex, hypothalamus, pituitary, adrenals, and gonads, and back to cortex. Could there be an asymmetrical relationship of the frontal cortex to the hypothalamic-pituitary-adrenal axis, as Robinson has shown for catecholamine neurotransmitters in the rat?

Robinson hypothesizes that the more frontal the lesion, the more effectively it will interrupt the noradrenergic axons, since they disperse as they pass from anterior to posterior. If he is correct, basal lesions that cut the noradrenergic pathway as it ascends to the frontal pole should be even more effective in producing depression. Evidence of this sort would be strong support for Robinson's idea.

DAVIDSON: EEG STUDIES OF EMOTION

Davidson was one of the first laterality researchers to investigate the possibility that the two hemispheres played different roles in affective behavior. He is one of the few studying the brain mechanisms involved in affect in normal people. Therefore, his observations can be very important as a foundation for understanding affective disorders in psychiatric or neurological populations. Like Robinson, he focuses on differences between right- and left-frontal regions and emphasizes anterior-posterior differences. We might look to studies like Davidson's to illuminate the mechanisms underlying the clinical phenomena that Robinson has described.

He has previously advanced the idea that all emotion could be divided into positive and negative and that the negative was in some way involved with the right hemisphere and the positive with the left. In many of his earlier experiments, the emotional stimuli were not differentiated except as "positive" and "negative," with these two terms rather undefined (see discussion above). In later work he began to ask whether or not the differences in frontal activation associated with affect applied to all emotions in each group. This has led in recent experiments to better and better specification of the emotions involved, as well as validation that they actually occurred. In this recent work he has studied sadness, fear, disgust, and some kinds of "happy." So far, these different emotions have been studied in different paradigms and with very different types of subjects, so it is still difficult to generalize about them or to make statements that apply to "negative" affects as a group. Sometimes authors use the terms negative or positive, implying a whole class of affects, in cases where the data only included a single affect.

From his review of the literature and his own results, Davidson concludes that the right hemisphere is superior in the *perception* of affective stimuli, for all emotions. However, with regard to experience and expression of emotion, he believes the approach/withdrawal dichotomy must be considered. Following up on an earlier suggestion of Kinsbourne's that the left hemisphere is involved with approach behavior and the right with withdrawal, Davidson proposes that to the extent that an emotion is associated with approach or withdrawal it will show lateralization. The classification of emotions with respect to approach and withdrawal is clear in some instances, e.g., disgust and fear. In his study with "method" actors, Davidson found disgust associated with right-frontal activation (alpha attenuation). In the case of sadness, the association is not so clear; there is longing for rapprochement with the lost object. There may be clinging or there may be stillness, but not withdrawal. In the actors' study, sadness was associated with a change in the proportion of right- to left-frontal alpha, but not a significant change in right-frontal activation considered by itself. There seems to be a piece of the puzzle missing here. Kinsbourne (Chapter 7) has refined his earlier "approach versus withdrawal" model to one of "continue-current-action versus arrest-action-and-rethink." This position may be more generally serviceable.

In Chapter 1 Davidson summarizes a large group of studies performed over the past decade that used both EEG and behavioral measures. For readers interested in more details, I highly recommend his theoretical review (Davidson 1984). Because this work is still in progress, there are many missing pieces, but Davidson does his best to make a coherent story out of the data presently in hand. I will comment only on the EEG studies. The points which seem most salient are these:

1. EEG can be used to study affective processes with high temporal resolution.
2. Asymmetries related to affective behavior are found in the frontal region, whereas asymmetries in the parietal region are related to other aspects of task and performance.
3. Frontal activation asymmetries associated with affective behavior are present in 10-month-old infants and even in newborns.
4. Greater relative activation of the right-frontal region is seen during facial expressions of disgust than during smiles. This very specific result is consistent with results of earlier experiments, in which subjects self-classified their affect simply as "positive" or "negative."
5. Individual differences in "resting" frontal asymmetry were predictive of subsequent responses to frightening stimuli in adults and infants. Those who showed greater fear responses had relatively greater right-frontal activation. However, EEG during the frightening experience did not distinguish between subjects with greater and lesser fear reactions.
6. Mildly depressed subjects could be distinguished from controls by their frontal asymmetry at rest. They showed relatively decreased left activation (not increased right activation).

There are many methodological strengths to this work. One is the variety of populations studied: normal adults, depressed students, "method" actors, and infants. Another is the variety of ways Davidson elicited emotional reactions: 1) watching films with terrifying, pleasant, disgusting, or sad content; 2) with the actors, imagining evocative situations; and with the infants, 3) looking at smiling and sad faces, 4) tasting pleasant and unpleasant substances, and 5) separation from their mothers and confrontation with strangers.

Another very important aspect of Davidson's method, used in two recent experiments, is the quantitative analysis of the facial expressions to indicate whether the emotion was actually elicited. The analysis of expressions also provided precise timing of *when* the emotion occurred, so that only that epoch of EEG could be examined.

This could be crucial, because no EEG differences were found during adjacent epochs in which no emotional expressions were occurring.

Contamination of the EEG by facial muscle potentials is another serious technical problem. Davidson handled this effectively by using high-frequency activity (70–80 Hz) in the EEG channel as an index of muscle activity; epochs in which activity in this band exceeded a modest criterion could be automatically rejected by the computer.

There are some problems of interpretation that apply to any EEG studies. The most basic one is the question of where the recorded signals are coming from. Davidson recorded from F3 and F4 with respect to a midline vertex reference, Cz. The pattern of activity observed can often be strongly affected by the choice of reference. For example, we have found that a midline reference is much better for demonstrating task-dependent alpha asymmetries than the more conventional linked-ears reference. Recently, the more complex "source derivation" reference method of Hjorth (Hjorth 1982; Thickbroom et al. 1984) has been recommended as giving the best spatial resolution, with less confounding by activity from the reference lead.

Even misattribution of the signal to the wrong hemisphere can occur; in the case of visually evoked potentials from the occipital region, for example, it is well known that visual stimulation of the activity in one hemisphere can cause larger evoked potentials over the opposite hemisphere because of the orientation of the dipoles of the striate cortex on the medial surface of the sagittal fissure (Jeffreys and Axford 1972; Blumhardt et al. 1978, 1982). This is unlikely in the present instance, but we must ask where in the frontal lobe the relevant activity is coming from. The frontal lobe has many subsystems; where else than right under the electrode might Davidson's alpha activity be coming from? Could activity related to approach and withdrawal be coming from the supplementary motor area on the medial surface of the sagittal fissure?

Another limitation on all EEG studies is the difficulty of measuring absolute levels of activity. Because absolute power differs from subject to subject by as much as 10 to 1 due to differences in skull thickness and other factors, we tend to use relative power measures: i.e., the within-subject ratio of power at one site to that at another, or the ratio of power in one condition to that in another. In the present studies, Davidson is usually reporting the *relative* power in one lead with respect to the power in the homologous lead. The reader must keep it in mind that an increase in relative right-frontal activation could be produced by a decrease in right-frontal alpha or by an increase in left-frontal alpha, or a little of both (e.g., Chapter 1, Table 3: "at-rest" ratios in babies who subsequently will or will not cry on separation from their mothers). Davidson *does* examine the levels of activity in each lead, not simply the right/left ratios; this information is generally available in his original journal publications.

The use of "relative" activation measures may intentionally or unintentionally carry with it the implication that what is functionally important is the balance between the two hemispheres. If the essential condition associated with sadness is activation of the right-frontal region *relative* to the left, rather than some *absolute* level of right activation, then that would explain why lesions that inactivated the left-frontal region are associated with "depression," as Starkstein and Robinson have found (Chapter 2). But it would also imply that subsequent right-frontal lesions would restore the balance and relieve the depression, and Robinson explicitly found that this was not so; it was the presence of left-frontal damage, regardless of the presence or absence of right-hemisphere damage, that correlated with depression. The data on relative therapeutic effectiveness of left, right, and bilateral electroconvulsive treatment (ECT) provides a parallel situation to that of the fixed lesions. In support of this idea, there is evidence that ECT to the right hemisphere is more effective in relieving depression than left-sided ECT (Galin 1974), but it is not clear that right ECT is more effective than bilateral.

In addition to expressing frontal activity on one side relative to the contralateral frontal region, frontal activity could be expressed relative to another ipsilateral region, e.g., the occipital or parietal region. Davidson has stressed the relationship of the frontal region to the ipsilateral parietal region, emphasizing reciprocal inhibition rather than other modes of interaction. It would be interesting to see if frontal activation level relative to parietal discriminated the various emotional conditions as well as, or differently than, the left-relative-to-right measures. Nevertheless, while I share Davidson's interest, it seems to me premature to build a model of affective behavior around the importance of reciprocal frontoparietal connections. First, I would like to see the present experiments extended to include recordings from the temporal lobes. Second, I would like to see an examination of the activity in bands other than alpha.

Overall, these results can be grouped into two sets, each potentially important, yet very difficult to integrate: first, the data showing the relation of frontal activation asymmetry to concurrent brief emotional reactions, and second, the data showing the relation of asymmetry during an affectively neutral "rest" condition to subsequent emotional reactions. Perhaps it depends on the particular emotion involved; the asymmetry was related to concurrent disgust, and the "resting" asymmetry was related to subsequent fear reactions. No current model accounts for such a difference. I would very much like to see these experiments simply repeated, without changes of the conditions or of the subject populations. We must await further results.

In the section titled "What Do Frontal Activation Asymmetries Reflect?" in Chapter 1, Davidson attempts to bring all the data together, proposing that "right-frontal activation is necessary but not sufficient for the experience of certain negative emotions." The word "necessary" seems unnecessarily strong; if that were so, patients with right-frontal lobectomies could not experience fear, sadness, and disgust. However, he then offers a more modest statement: "The presence of right-frontal activation might represent a 'vulnerability' for the experience of negative emotion. The threshold for eliciting negative affect might be lower. . . ." He is planning further experiments to specifically test whether this "vulnerability" is related to the appraisal process, the affect program itself, or coping responses. This seems to me an interesting formulation and a productive opening for research.

FINSET: MOOD DISORDER FOLLOWING RIGHT-HEMISPHERE DAMAGE

Two features distinguish Finset's chapter for me. First, he emphasizes the richness of qualitative differences among the affect disorders following brain damage, rather than dichotomizing into depressed versus euphoric or catastrophic reaction versus indifference reaction. Second, he thoughtfully addresses the treatment implications of his neuropsychological analysis.

Finset explicitly talks about mood as distinct from thought content and vegetative symptoms. This must be kept in mind when trying to integrate his results with others, such as Robinson, who uses the Zung, Hamilton, and Present State Examination scales, which combine these symptoms into a single score.

In two studies of right-hemisphere damage, Finset found greater mood depression with posterior than with anterior lesions, as did Robinson (except for one study: Robinson et al. 1984a). Unfortunately, details about the lesions are not presented. It should be remembered that Sinyor et al. (1986) found a curvilinear relationship between depression and distance of the lesion from the frontal pole, i.e., severe depression with lesions far anterior as well as posterior. Their sample included cases with lesions further anterior than those studied by Robinson.

Twice in his chapter Finset makes the point that severity of mood depression was related to the depth of the lesion, not only to the anterior-posterior location. Patients with pure cortical lesions over the parietal region showed only a low degree of depressed mood. At last a blow against cortical chauvinism! This is an extremely important observation. What were the subcortical structures involved? Recall that in Robinson's animal work the effects on neurotransmitters and hyperactivity were produced by lesions restricted to the cortex.

Finset develops the suggestion of Kinsbourne and Bemporad (1984) that there might be qualitative differences between the depressions following left-anterior and right-posterior strokes. He finds the right-hemisphere cases to have a "diffusely depressed mood," characterized by sad subjective state, looking sad, and "a certain degree of inertia," with little depressive thought content and, particularly, few suicidal ideas. He also found them to show little anxiety or vegetative signs. This is very different from the picture drawn by Gainotti of depressions following left-hemisphere lesions.

Right-hemisphere lesions, including posterior ones, are famous for being associated with "indifference reactions" rather than depressed mood (Gainotti 1972), and it is not clear why some patients show indifference and some show depressed mood. It is not simply that one is being mistaken for the other; Finset finds that *within his right-lesioned population* there is a significant negative correlation between indifference symptoms and depressed mood measures. Perhaps the differences here are due to social and psychodynamic factors superimposed on the common organic deficit.

Both groups share a lack of initiative, difficulty with concentration, and what Finset terms "reduced emotionality." This quality of reduced emotionality seems very interesting to me; it might be useful to distinguish whether the patients with this symptom have difficulty grasping the emotional meaning of a stimulus situation or if they have a decreased ability to react to it even though they understand it, and whether the former is associated with posterior lesions and the latter with anterior lesions. In terms of the Ekman affect model discussed above, do they have a difficulty with appraisal or with releasing the affect program?

CONCLUSION

At the beginning of this chapter, I asserted that this volume in general addresses the question, "What can we say about the brain mechanisms related to depression?" This led us to inquire into what we mean by affect, affective disorder, and depression. We considered the pitfalls of naive localizationism and some more sophisticated current neuropsychological models. With these definitions and models in mind, we then examined some data at very different levels of analysis: some

EEG data on activity in the frontal and parietal regions during affective behavior in normal people and the effects on affective behavior of lesions in different parts of the brain. In the course of this examination, many issues came up that I believe are relevant to the other chapters in this volume.

What points should stay with us?

1. It is possible to study affect in a rigorous way, at several different levels of analysis.
2. To account for the complexity of affective processes (and depression in particular), we need dynamic models based on interactions between psychological subsystems and also between brain subsystems, rather than static models based on centers, traits, or titers of vital humours.
3. In research on mechanisms in depression, the cognitive, affective, and vegetative components should be differentiated.
4. The two hemispheres play different roles in affective behavior. How we understand these different roles will depend on the models of affect that we develop.
5. The locus of a brain lesion contributes to its affective consequences—not only left/right but anterior/posterior and cortical/subcortical.
6. The particulars of the life of the individual in whom the brain lesion occurs also contribute to the affective consequences of that lesion.

A comprehensive neuropsychological understanding of depression requires elements from many levels of analysis: anatomical distinctions, such as hypothalamus versus forebrain and anterior versus posterior cortex; short-acting neurotransmitters such as norepinephrine and dopamine versus long-acting neuroendocrine modulators such as cortisol; behavioral factors such as the degree of disability and consequent disruption of life that must be coped with; and psychodynamic factors such as the organization of the personality that must do the coping. We are emerging from the confusion of single-cause or single-level thinking, such as "it's a frontal problem," "it's a catecholamine problem," "it's an adrenal steroid problem," "it's a cognitive problem," or "it's an intrapersonal psychodynamic problem." This volume illustrates our real progress at each level and the beginnings of integration.

REFERENCES

Bogen JE, Bogen GM: The other side of the brain, III: the corpus callosum and creativity. Bull Los Angeles Neurol Soc 34:191–220, 1969

Bower GH: Mood and memory. Am Psychol 36:129–148, 1981

Bower GH: Affect and cognition. Philos Trans R Soc Lond [Biol] 302:387–402, 1983

Blumhardt LD, Barret G, Halliday AM, et al: The effect of experimental scotomata on the ipsilateral and contralateral responses to pattern-reversal in one half-field. Electroencephalography and Clinical Neurophysiology 45:376–392, 1978

Blumhardt LD, Barret G, Kriss A, et al: The pattern-evoked potential in lesions of the posterior visual pathways. Ann NY Acad Sci 388:264–289, 1982

Davidson RJ: Affect, cognition, and hemispheric specialization, in Emotion, Cognition, and Behavior. Edited by Izard CE, Kagan J, Zajonc R. New York, Cambridge University Press, 1984

Ekman P: Biological and cultural contributions to body and facial movement, in The Anthropology of the Body. Edited by Blacking J. London, Academic Press, 1977

Ekman P: Expression and the nature of emotion, in Approaches to Emotion. Edited by Scherer K, Ekman P. Hillsdale, NJ, Erlbaum, 1984

Ekman P, Friesen WV: Unmasking the Face. Palo Alto, CA, Consulting Psychologists Press, 1975

Gainotti G: Emotional behavior and hemispheric side of the lesion. Cortex 8:41–55, 1972

Galin D: Implications for psychiatry of left and right cerebral specialization: a neurophysiological context for unconscious processes. Arch Gen Psychiatry 31:572–583, 1974

Galin D: Two modes of consciousness and the two halves of the brain, in Symposium on Consciousness. Edited by Lee PR, Ornstein RE, Galin D, et al. New York, Viking Press, 1976

Galin D: Lateral specialization and psychiatric issues: speculations on the development and evolution of consciousness. Ann NY Acad Sci 299:397–411, 1977

Galin D, Johnstone J, Nakell L, et al: Development of the capacity for tactile information transfer between hemispheres in normal children. Science 204:1330–1332, 1979

Goldberg G: Supplementary motor area structure and function: review and hypotheses. Behavioral and Brain Sciences 8:567–616, 1985

Hellige J: Cerebral Hemisphere Asymmetry: Method, Theory, and Application. New York, Praeger, 1983

Hjorth B: An adaptive EEG derivation technique. EEG Clin Neurophysiol 54:654-661, 1982

Izard CE: Human Emotion. New York, Plenum, 1977

Jeffreys DA, Axford JG: Source locations of pattern-specific components of human visual evoked potentials, I: Component of striate cortical origin. Exp Brain Res 16:1–21, 1972

Kinsbourne M, Bemporad B: Lateralization of emotion: a model and the evidence, in Psychology of Affective Development. Edited by Fox NA, Davidson RJ. Hillsdale, NJ, Erlbaum, 1984

Mandler G: Mind and Body: Psychology of Emotion and Stress. New York, Norton, 1984

Milner B, Petrides M: Behavioral effects of frontal lobe lesions in man. Trends in Neurosciences 7:403–407, 1984

Pearlson GD, Kubos KL, Robinson RG: Effect of anterior-posterior lesion location on the asymmetrical behavioral and biochemical response to cortical suction ablations in the rat. Brain Res 293:241–250, 1984

Rhoades HM, Overall JE: The Hamilton Depression Scale: factor scoring and profile classification. Psychopharmcol Bull 19:91–96, 1983

Robinson RG: Differential behavioral and biochemical effects of right and left hemispheric cerebral infarction in the rat. Science 205:707–710, 1979

Robinson RG, Szetela B: Mood change following left hemispheric brain injury. Ann Neurol 9:447–453, 1981

Robinson RG, Starr LB, Kubos KL, et al: A two-year longitudinal study of post-stroke mood disorders: findings during the initial evaluation. Stroke 14:736–741, 1983

Robinson RG, Starr LB, Lipsey JR, et al: A two-year longitudinal study of post-stroke mood disorders: dynamic changes in associated variables over the first six months of follow-up. Stroke 15:510–516, 1984a

Robinson RG, Kubos KL, Starr LB, et al: Mood disorders in stroke patients. Brain 107:81–93, 1984b

Robinson RG, Starr LB, Lipsey JR, et al: A two-year longitudinal study of post-stroke mood disorders: in-hospital prognostic factors associated with six-month outcome. J Nerv Mental Dis 173:221–226, 1985

Roland PE: Metabolic measurements of the working frontal cortex in man. Trends in Neuroscience 7:430–435, 1984

Ross ED, Rush AJ: Diagnosis and neuroanatomical correlates of depression in brain-damaged patients. Arch Gen Psychiatry 38:1344–1354, 1981

Sinyor D, Jacques P, Kaloupek DG, et al: Post-stroke depression and lesion location, an attempted replication. Brain 109:537–546, 1986

Sprague J: Interaction of cortex and superior colliculus in mediation of visually guided behavior in the cat. Science 153:1544–1547, 1966

Starr LB, Robinson RG, Price TR: Reliability, validity, and clinical utility of the social functioning exam in the assessment of stroke patients. Exp Aging Res 9:101–106, 1983

Thickbroom GW, Mastaglia FL, Carroll WM, et al: Source derivation: application to topographic mapping of visual evoked potentials. Electroencephalography and Clinical Neurophysiology 59:279–285, 1984

Tomkins SS: Affect as amplification; some modification in theory, in Emotion: Theory, Research, and Application. Edited by Plutchik R, Kellerman H. New York, Academic Press, 1980

Wexler BE: A model of brain function: its implications for psychiatric research. Br J Psychiatry 149:202–209, 1986

Zaidel E: Disconnection syndrome as a model for laterality effects in the normal brain, in Cerebral Hemisphere Asymmetry: Method, Theory, and Application. Edited by Hellige J. New York, Praeger, 1983